Spirit AUTOBIOGRAPHY OF A PSYCHIC MEDIUM *Whispers*

Charmaine Wilson

FONTAINE
—PRESS—

Copyright © Charmaine Wilson

First published in 2006
Published in 2009 by Fontaine Press
P.O. Box 948, Fremantle
Western Australia 6959
www.fontainepress.com

National Library of Australia Cataloguing-in-Publication data
Author: Wilson, Charmaine, 1964-
Title: Spirit whispers : autobiography of a psychic medium
        / Charmaine Wilson.
Edition: 2nd rev. ed.
ISBN: 9780980417098 (pbk.)
Subjects: Wilson, Charmaine.
            Mediums--Australia--Biography.
Dewey Number: 133.91092

For more information about the author,
please visit: www.spiritwhispers.org

Acknowledgements

Since winning Channel Seven's *The One: The Search for Australia's Most Gifted Psychic*, many aspects of my life have changed; so have the format and layout of *Spirit Whispers*, my first book originally published in 2006.

Spirit Whispers is my first foray into writing and is a part of my journey that made me who I am today. For that reason, the story remains the same as it was in the previous edition.

Life is a journey of highs and lows that affect all of us differently, depending on our level of learning. The young medium I was when I wrote *Spirit Whispers* has matured.

The road I have travelled has twisted and turned. I have met many along the way who have played their part in my life and moved on.

Many good friends still remain and for this I am thankful, but it would be remiss of me to ever forget those who have helped me along the way.

I will always be thankful of my Spirit guide, Peter, the patient one, and of my small army of spirit helpers that lead me to the right place at the right time.

My spirit family is never far from me and has recently called my mother home. To Mum, Dad, Martin, Grandpop, Grandma and my beautiful spirit daughter, Crystal – for eternity we travel – till we meet again in the next life.

Your spirits are a constant source of comfort to me.

Without the support of my living family, I would be a mess. I doubt I would still be sane. I am better for having them in my life. To my new family, Patrick and co – my love to you.

My closest friends, Debbie and Trevor, Ezio and Michelle, Sue and Ron, Herman, Rebmen, thank you for keeping me close.

To the countless business associates who have patiently worked by my side and shown the ropes, you are all Gods of your trades. A very special thank you to John Schuur.

The media are my friends – The Two Davids – love you both.

To all the radio stations across Australia – thank you.

To all the people and friends who voted for me, believed in me and made my dream of working with the bereaved parents a reality – The spirit children and I thank you.
I hope you all understand how much you mean to me and I hope I mean the same to you.

Foreword

The spiritual path isn't always a pretty one. We hope it ends up for the best sooner rather than later of course, but the travel towards our higher good, especially at first, is often littered with tragic mistakes, and for some, with outright danger. It is because of the seemingly ugly face of change that many of us stop, give up prematurely, never to find that place in our lives where what we deeply wanted was realised.

In these times where there is a New Age store in every mall and a guru on every corner, getting 'spiritual' has never been easier. A crystal here, a smudge stick there, and it is easy to think that you are authentically a much more conscious spiritual being.

However, it's my experience that the most authentic of spiritual paths involves a lot more than a few books and a wind chime or two. Walking your walk and not just talking 'the' talk often means massive changes in how you live your life and that decision to change for the long term is an incredibly brave one.

You may lose partners, friends, your job, habits, even your old identity. You might make huge mistakes, hit rock bottom, claw your way back up… all in the hope that you are transforming into something better. Something that you *really want*. Charmaine Wilson demonstrates that this bravery is worth it.

The story you are about to read is often harrowing, yet one of great hope. It's about an ordinary woman who has an extraordinary experience. It shows that you too can change and grow no matter what. It has a phoenix-like quality and encourages those that read it to rise from their personal ashes, heal and start afresh. You don't have to believe in spirits. You don't have to believe in ghosts. In fact, you don't have to even believe that mediums really do talk to the dead to be affected by it.

However, if you do have an open mind or do believe in the kind of spirit world that Charmaine communicates with, well, this story has yet another greater level of meaning. It means that those that pass from this world of the living still choose to love and communicate with those that are still here. These communications, for many, give great comfort and ease from the deep sorrow of missing them...and Charmaine is a channel for these messages.

A great responsibility.

A great gift.

And a story worth reading.

Stacey Demarco
Metaphysicist, Witch, Educator and Author of *Witch in the Boardroom*, *Witch in the Bedroom* and *The Coffee Oracle*.
www.themodernwitch.com

Have you seen a rainbow fall from the sky?
Did you see that angel lose her wings?
Do you think that she will die?
Have you watched your dreams disappear
down into a blood red sea?
Are you asking me if these things have affected me?

CRYSTAL SHEREE WILSON   4 ½ YEARS
13 NOVEMBER, 1981 - 28 JUNE 1986
LOVED FOREVER

I have waited almost twenty years to stand in this spot. I have cried oceans of tears over this small blue cross, yet this is the first time I've ever seen it. Strangely, the pain accumulated over nearly two decades dissolves instantly into annoyance. They have misspelled "Charee"!

It's been a long journey to this point. Even to be able to stand in the town that claimed my young daughter's life is a huge step for me. This town of Kempsey, on the New South Wales coastline. This place where my girl was both conceived and taken. The events that happened here abruptly changed my life, sending me spiralling into the depths of hell before I woke up to find myself on one of the most amazing rides anyone could imagine.

So, here I stand at last and there it is. A little blue cross standing on its own at the back of the East Kempsey Cemetery, with my beautiful little girl's name misspelled. If anyone had consulted me or included me in her burial they would have known the correct spelling. I just shake my head. My whole life had been like this, really − everything was always a bit off balance, always walking the wrong walk and stepping way over the normal boundaries of society. I used to take it all so personally, punishing myself for every misstep, every wrong turn. Now I know better. I am just myself and every step on this journey has brought me here....

Chapter 1

Early Days

Some say that psychics are born, not made. I'm not sure whether they're right or not, but as a child I was not aware of my psychic abilities, although in hindsight there were signs of things to come. Perhaps the facility is there for everyone and life's events either give us reason to open those doors, or they don't. Perhaps certain people are destined from the beginning to experience life in such a way that spirit has an opportunity to work through them. All I know is that everything I have been through in my life has led me to where I am today, and I believe that I am where I was destined to be.

When I was born, my brother Martin really wanted a little brother, so instead of my chosen name, Charmaine, he called me George. My earliest memory is of Martin sleepwalking and waking me up from a deep sleep. I remember being frightened that there was someone in my room. Martin simply curled up on the end of my bed and continued sleeping. According to my mother we were very close, so close that I barely spoke a word until I was four. My brother spoke for me, always telling mum of my precise needs, never getting it wrong. It was not until he went to preschool that I finally found my voice. In hindsight, I've often wondered if we were telepathic, but as a child it just seemed normal to me.

We lived in Ingham, North Queensland, and the house was always filled with the scent of mangoes; mango chutney to be precise. My Grandpop, Mervyn, boiled up enough chutney to sink a battleship. Grandpop's was such a strong brew; our house was virtually fermented with the smell of the stuff. He used to hand it out to all the local barmaids and shop owners as gifts, but they eventually handed it back because he had made it too spicy for human consumption! Back into the pot it would all go, with Grandpop adding even more mangoes to make it edible. To this day, I cannot eat mangoes. It was all too much for a five-year-old.

My parents divorced when I was five, and we travelled in Grandpop's old Holden from Ingham to Brisbane, where we caught a train to Sydney. A week later, Grandpop sent the cat and the bird via train to us. He had put the cat in a pine fruit box and nailed the lid down. When mum opened the lid, she found a string of cheerios (little red cocktail sausages) in the box with the cat. It turned out that Grandpop had forgotten to put food in the box before he nailed it shut, and the cheerios were the only things he could push through the holes! Needless to say, they lay untouched in the box when the cat arrived in Sydney... We moved around a fair bit, as mum settled into her new life. I remember the song *Bridge Over Troubled Waters* by Simon and Garfunkel was a hit at the time. As young as I was, I would cry when I heard it. It was our song, Martin's and mine. It always reminds me of those days when we clung together as children in a new place. Mum got a job in a service station where she met John, my stepfather. John was perhaps the first person to open my mind to the possibility of other dimensions. As a seven-year-old, I would listen spellbound as he related his theories of ghosts and alien life. John was also a talented artist and he painted mum's old car bright blue with flowers all over it. Very fitting for the era! We first moved to Bankstown as a family and before too long, our new brother, Patrick, arrived and things began to settle down again. I was always eager to help out and loved to wash up at my mum's friends' houses. Mum would sit and chat with her friends and I would virtually polish the kitchen whilst they did so. I was always a welcome visitor.

Mum was a bad asthmatic so we had to do a lot more housework than our peers, and we did it whining and arguing all the way. We fought constantly. At her wit's end, Mum would threaten to tell John when he came home. It didn't deter us even though she always made good with the threats. Martin was always first to 'get the belt' and I would lie on my bed, terrified, waiting for my turn. Martin would scream blue murder even before you heard the belt connect, but I wasn't quite so smart. I would hold stubbornly, refusing to make a single sound until it really hurt. Very often, this meant I'd cop twice the hiding Martin did. It was traumatic, but not uncommon in those times for fathers to dish out similar punishments. We just accepted it. Most of the time, I was a very good and quiet little girl - when my brother wasn't around. There was an area down in our backyard where Martin told me some kids had burnt to death because they were playing with matches. Of course, I believed him and kept away. I believed everything my brother told me. I was such a gullible and open child. He would torment me constantly, always teasing and threatening me in the way big brothers often do. I now believe he was my greatest teacher throughout my childhood and teenage years. Even so, I think I may possibly have been the most tea towel-flicked sister in the world. Life was complicated and there were always issues, but through it all, Martin and I always referred to each other as the 'real sibling' and we stuck together no matter what.

The other constant in my life was Grandpop, who also lived in Sydney at the time. He was always up to mischief and seemed so full of life to me. I knew that nothing bad could ever happen as long as he was around. He went on a cruise to Fiji when I was about seven and we all went to look at the cruise ship. I was so envious! My imagination was fuelled by his adventures and I remember feeling like a pirate princess when he brought me back some exotic necklaces made of apple seeds.

Some of my best memories of my grandfather are from Bankstown in the 1970s. He was funny in a typical Australian way. He used to drive to the pub and I would wait in the car while he drank inside. He would come out at regular intervals with a soft drink and chips and make sure I was ok. On the drive home one night, I kept hearing these little 'bump bump bump' noises. I looked out the window and saw that the noise was coming from the wheels as we drove over the lane markers in the middle of the highway.

"Grandpop, why are those little things in the middle of the road?" I asked, as he ran over them again - 'bump bump bump'.

"That's how you know that you're driving on the wrong side of the road," Grandpop informed me. Unaware that there might have been better ways, I accepted his answer and settled back down in my seat, as the car swerved merrily all over Princess Highway.

I guess you could say that I had a few 'near death experiences' as a passenger in Grandpop's car! I know now how lucky I was not to have been involved in an accident, but as a little girl it never occurred to me that someone who loved me as much as Grandpop did would put me in harm's way. Grandpop eventually had to leave Sydney when he sideswiped sixteen cars in one go after a night at the pub. He came home, hitched up the caravan and drove all the way back to Queensland.

I was a quiet child and much preferred the characters in my books to real people. Once, I heard Grandpop comment to mum that it was unhealthy for me to be in my room reading all the time. But I didn't care what they said. Enid Blyton caught me up in tales of fairies and gnomes. I was spellbound at the possibility that there was a fairy kingdom and that little people really did exist. In fact, I was convinced they did. After all, I had seen things...

I can clearly remember one occasion when a man, whom I suspected was a ghost, came and sat on the end of my bed. He was quite old and I was more than a little scared though I knew instinctively that he meant no harm. He just sat there and looked at me and then just as quickly as he came, he left. I thought he might have been related to my stepfather, but because I was not sure if he had really been there at all, I kept quiet. If Martin had known, he would have teased me, so I kept these kinds of secrets between me and my dog. I loved all animals and would despair at hurting one single thing, even an ant. I had begged and begged mum for a dog, so she took me to an animal shelter to choose one. Mum had her eye on a nice little dachshund who was very cute. She was quite dismayed when I picked the ugliest mongrel there because I felt sorry for him. We called him Pooch and I spent many hours under the mulberry tree telling him of my childhood woes. The days of Enid Blyton, mulberry trees and sharing secrets with Pooch came to an end when my father lost a leg in an accident involving a drunken friend. In 1975, when I was nine years old, we moved up to Brisbane to start a new life and Dad moved to Brisbane as well. In many respects, I left my childhood behind.

I was amazed at how laid-back the schools were in Queensland compared to what I had been used to. At Yagoona we wore ties and black school shoes - at Ormiston they wore *thongs*. It was such a culture shock for me. The kids were wilder and I was determined to fit right in. I learned how to climb a tree and promptly and embarrassingly got stuck in it. I had already developed a strong love for music, but now I began to enjoy much raunchier tones than any eleven-year-old should. The Sweet was big at that time as were Alice Cooper and Led Zeppelin, and I started to turn the volume right up. I forgot about Enid Blyton and smoked my first cigarette at eleven, convinced it was cool to be bad.

Of course, to my brother I could never be cool – and he felt he had the market cornered in terms of badness. He was happy to demonstrate his excellent techniques at every opportunity, inventing many creative ways to torture and humiliate me. One particular incident sticks out from that time. My father was always a very determined person and with one leg or two, he would do his leatherwork and take it to the markets. Martin and I would help him when we spent weekends there. I had a horrific cold one day when we were doing some leatherwork for him and my sniffling was driving Martin mad. Menacing me with a stud gun, my dear brother demanded I blow my nose into a plastic bag. It was totally disgusting and just the sort of humiliation that Martin enjoyed dishing out! Of course, he told as many people as he could, which didn't help me much in the cool stakes. Luckily, I had other charms up my sleeve. The boys thought I was beautiful and I was becoming very popular for all the wrong reasons. Time moves on and kids turn into teenagers. My own teenage transformation left behind little trace of the quiet withdrawn girl I had once been. My middle name changed from Ann to Trouble, with a capital T.

By this time, Grandpop was back on the scene. Of course, I had grown up a lot and my attitude towards him had changed. In the way that most grandfathers annoy their teenage granddaughters, he annoyed me. I'd bake a cake and leave it to cool so I could ice it, and come back to find Grandpop had snaffled about a third of it off to his caravan. Dinnertime was always a circus. My stepfather would eat his steak raw, so I would make a barricade of sauce bottles and saltshakers to avoid any possibility of seeing his dinner stand right up and 'moo' at me. Martin complained loudly that we all munched like disgusting pigs and would often take his dinner to the phone table to spare his delicate sensibilities. I'd be left at the table between John's gory plate load and Grandpop. Every time I'd blink or look the other way, Grandpop would pinch the juiciest piece of meat or roast potatoes right off my plate. Now, I liked my roast potatoes - I still do - but so did Grandpop and there was no stopping him.

He infuriated me, but always made me laugh. Eventually, Grandpop had to leave the area when he reversed straight out of the driveway and smacked into a parked car that belonged to a Jehovah's Witness. True to form, Grandpop drove back up the driveway, hitched up his caravan and hightailed it to the Sunshine Coast where he stayed until he was convinced the coast was clear.

I was desperate to fit in at high school. Yes, it was cool to be bad, but what I was really looking for was love, acceptance, a sense of belonging and being an important part of something. If that was going to come from hormone-enriched boys and friends who smoked, drank and lied to their parents, so be it! I was up for anything. Although I acted streetwise, inside I just felt lost and sad. My school friend, Joanne, remembers how obviously sensitive and emotionally open I was at the time, which was a recipe for disaster in that environment. The wholesome worlds created by Enid Blyton certainly seemed very, very far away. After all, it was the late 70's - currant buns and fairies really had no place in an era of punk rock and casual sex. Joanne had moved to the area around the same time as I had and was as lost in her environment as I was. We had sleepovers occasionally, giggling ourselves sick and comparing notes about boys, the perils of vile older brothers – and boys.

On one of those occasions, we thought it might be fun to experiment with a makeshift ouija board. Who or what we intended to communicate with, I don't know, but under our trembling teenage hands, the cup spelled out all kinds of specific and frightening things. Jo thought *I* was moving the cup and I thought *she* was moving the cup. At one point, my cat Marmaduke wandered into the room, hissed like a demon and tore off again like the hounds from hell were chasing him. Scary stuff! To this day we don't know what was moving the cup, but we scared ourselves rigid that night and I cowered in the corner, absolutely terrified and refusing to speak until my parents came home. It was all too real for me. After this introductory foray into the world of ouija, we backed off from any further psychic experiments. My brother, Martin, had a crush on Jo all through high school and they dated on-and-off for some time, which made maintaining our friendship awkward at times. Most of my adventures depended on Martin knowing nothing about my after-school activities. After all, he still had the power to make sure I 'got the belt' and he wasn't afraid to use it. Joanne's father died in 1977 and not long afterwards, she left the school and we lost touch for many years.

I was a very social teenager who had many friends and used my days at school to socialise. My best friend in high-school was Marjon Kok, who had the most disgusting brother, Dirk. My first day at high school, nice and fresh in my new school uniform, was when I met Dirk as he wiped his blood nose all down my sleeve. I was very upset and turned to the girl next to me as we sat waiting for instructions when I spied him again.

"See that boy? He is a pig!"

To which Marjon replied, "That's my brother and yes, he *is* a pig!"

A friendship was formed for life.

Another friend I had for many years was Hope.

My friend Hope had the lying-to-the-parents factor down to a fine art, and a passion for bad boys on motor-bikes to match my own, so I gravitated towards her and together we went off the rails. I got drunk for the first time at fourteen and went on to try nearly all types of recreational drugs, always looking for a quick fix for the unsettled feeling I had inside. Hope was never far away and we egged each other on to try new experiences and break new rules. Martin and I kept up our fighting schedule without a break, often having screaming matches at school in front of the whole crowd. He was by no means an angel, but still he watched my every move and anything I did wrong was either held over my head for blackmail purposes or reported in detail to our parents. I was in fact a brilliant student, streamed into the advanced maths class and the top commercial class, and I always received best marks at school. Even so, I was spinning out of control and was eventually expelled from high school in the ninth grade for inappropriate behaviour consisting of smoking, vandalism and leaving the school grounds on the back of a motorbike. At fifteen I met a boy called Tony Wilson, fell pregnant to him at the ripe old age of sixteen and was married ten days after my seventeenth birthday. I guess that was one way to avoid 'the belt'.

Surprisingly, my greatest ally at this time was Martin. From the beginning of my pregnancy, he began to soften towards me. At this time, he was working as a cabinetmaker and he couldn't bear to see me sleeping on the floor, so he made me a queen-size waterbed from scratch. Dad, who had a furniture business at the time, supplied the materials. I felt very special. My daughter Crystal Charee was born at 4.34 pm on the 13th of November 1981 - Black Friday. My life changed from the moment I laid eyes on her. At last, I had found someone to love who would love me unconditionally. I calculated that I would only be thirty-five when she would turn eighteen. In those first glowing moments, I anticipated all the happy years ahead.

Mum, Grandpop, Tony and of course my brother were all smitten with this wonderful new life. The day Martin first met Crystal is a day I have never forgotten. As he held my tiny girl in his arms, he visibly softened and I think he fell deeply in love. The animosity that surrounded our teenage years dissolved and at last a warm friendship developed between us that I will always cherish. When I brought Crystal home, Martin became a constant visitor and actually made my couch his home. He would drive me crazy, drinking all my milk and eating all my food, but he was my brother and when he was driving me nuts, I would just picture him with Crystal the day she was born. He was very proud of her and would often bring his noisy mates home to visit his niece. The love was definitely a two-way thing. Crystal would quite often just stare at him with fascination. I think Martin had discovered in Crystal the same thing I had: unconditional love. We were still unsettled, Martin and I, but maybe it was never too late to teach an old dog new tricks.

Chapter 2

Loss: The Journey Begins

When I was 17 years old, I didn't know what a medium was nor had I experienced grief. I was married, the mother of a four-month-old baby girl named Crystal Charee, and my future lay ahead of me as it does for any 17-year-old – full of big dreams and unlimited potential. Life had not been a bed of roses to this point, but on this fine day, April 2nd 1982, I was feeling very happy. Despite the trials and tribulations that face every new mother, my life was better than it had been for a long time and I had reasons to be optimistic.

My brother Martin had slept on the couch (again) and unfortunately had asthma when he awoke. For some reason, instead of our usual non-morning-people argument, I was feeling very loving toward Martin and even offered him my asthma puffer to take to work. Martin was excited about moving in with his girlfriend that day, asking me to look after her motorcycle helmet. He said he would be by that afternoon to collect it. I watched from the door as he rode off and for the first time ever, he turned around and waved. In that split second my mind took a photo which has never left me. Every detail remains intact.

Crystal and I were going shopping with my mother. As we got ready, the radio reported a fatal accident close by.

I briefly wondered if it had involved anyone I knew, but quickly put the news out of my mind. We went shopping as planned and I bought Crystal her very first Easter chocolate egg. I couldn't resist giving her the egg when we arrived back at mum's and was laughing at her obvious enjoyment of this strange new treasure as we walked through the front door. My stepfather met me with a grim expression that wiped the smile right off my face. He told me to sit down and then broke the news. Martin had been killed instantly in a bike accident only 10km from his home. A car had failed to stop at the stop sign.

For the first time in my life, I experienced the devastating shockwave of tragic death. I know that I screamed and I will never forget the sheer panic, desperation and grief that I felt in that first minute. Every part of me was screaming 'NO' except one, that small part of me that knew it was true. It was like I had fallen into a nightmare – instant overwhelming agony on every level. That day, I wanted to crawl out of my own skin to escape the pain. I found myself watching a news report on the accident later in the evening. Funny how we tend to remember odd details of such moments. I remember noticing that Martin's boots had landed in different positions on the road. Only the day or so beforehand, he had complained that they were too big. His bike, his pride and joy, was nothing but a chocolate-brown tangled mess. Also filmed at the scene was the ambulance that held the corpse of my brother. He was just 20 years old.

The days that followed were incredibly blurry. I could not open my eyes without the tears flowing like from a tap. My brother, my 'real sibling', my daughter's adoring uncle, my childhood tormentor and friend was gone.

Just like that. How often had I said to him when I was a child and knew no better, that I wished he were dead? I remembered quite clearly telling Martin that I was going to grow older than him. I think I was about eight at the time. It was a shock when I remembered those prophetic words after his death, and in my immaturity, I wondered if I had somehow contributed to his early demise by even uttering those words. I experienced a constant rollercoaster ride of denial, grief, tears, pain, guilt and anger. It was like trying to stand still in the surf. Every emotion just kept rushing at me over and over, like giant powerful breakers, and it was impossible to keep my footing. I felt helplessness beyond belief that nothing, not one thing in this world could fill the enormous hole that had just been torn open inside my heart. I had never been affectionate towards any of my relatives and now it was all too late. How could I tell him I loved him now? How could I tell him anything? Where was he? Was he safe? Could he hear me? Questions, questions and more questions formed in my mind, but there were no answers. The 'whys', the 'if-onlys' and the 'buts' just kept on coming, but there was nothing. Just grief - raw, painful and relentless. Every day when I opened my eyes, the rollercoaster revved up again.

Martin's funeral was massive. There were people there that I had not seen since high school. There must have been about 300 people - maybe more, maybe less. It was hard to tell through the veil of tears. We decided to view the body, just to make sure in our minds that it was Martin we were saying goodbye to. It's a cliché, but he did look very peaceful - quite serene in fact, with a strange Mona Lisa smile on his face. He was definitely not 'there' though. It was only his body we saw that day, and it hurt like hell. Still, those of us who were the closest to Martin got through the experience the best way they could. We all drank and smoked too much. We even dragged out the old ouija board, which had us convinced we had made contact. But still, we grieved. As the days and weeks passed, I wrote poetry and songs to try to express my feelings.

To My Brother

When they told me your brother's dead,
I can't remember what I said.
I remember thinking it can't be true,
I remember how the sky was blue.

It doesn't seem fair to take you away,
I know you didn't have your way
All you wanted was to have fun and be free,
No one knew that this is how it would be.

I watched the news the night you died,
I saw your helmet, I saw your bike
I saw the ambulance in which you lay,
All I could do was cry and cry.

I am sorry for all the things I said,
I only wish it were me instead
And I wouldn't have to feel this pain,
Of knowing I'll never see you again.

Charmaine, April 1982

Hour after hour, day after day, week after week and year after year, the stream of questions remained unanswered. In 1982, mediums were not common in Australia. Looking back, Doris Stokes was perhaps the only famous one, but she was not well publicised and it just didn't occur to any of us that there might be somebody out there who could provide the answers we so desperately needed. So we just grieved.

* * *

Two years later, I separated from Crystal's father. Tony had been a fixture in my life for a long time – his wild and woolly blond hair and his nutty sense of humour had always melted my heart. We had made a beautiful daughter together and had tried to do what was expected of us as a young family, but Tony was a heavy drinker and in the end, I just couldn't cope. I think the truth is we outgrew each other. When we separated, Tony went back to coastal New South Wales to live with his parents and I moved in with a friend.

I had full custody of Crystal, but I really did feel for Tony as I knew how much he adored his daughter. We wanted to be fair to each other, keeping what was best for Crystal as the first priority. After all, she loved us both and it wasn't her fault that we couldn't get on as a married couple. As she was only two and a half years old, we arranged to share as much time as possible with her between us, at least until she started school. We agreed that I would have her for two months and then she would spend one month with her father and grandparents in New South Wales. This arrangement worked quite well.

My mother and I took turns calling Crystal on alternate days and sent lots of letters and postcards while she was there.

By 1985, Crystal and I were living alone in our own little 'nest'. We had settled into a routine and I had begun to pick up the threads of a social life, now that I was single again. One night at a party, I met an attractive 26-year-old named Mick – and instantly fell head-over-heels for him. Mick rode a motorbike and for me, he had the right look, words and attitude. His 'take-charge' manner made me feel safe. With a look from Mick, I felt like a schoolgirl again. He made me feel beautiful, sexy and alive. I pursued him - and he ran - but we couldn't stay away from each other for long. We were mates and I felt very loved. In May 1986, Mick moved in with us.

Mick and I were both heavy drinkers and regulars on the local party scene at the time. Looking back, I can see we were both trying a bit too hard to have fun. I was still recovering from Martin's death and the break-up of my marriage, and Mick was grieving the loss of a child some years before. After a complicated birth resulting in severe brain damage, Mick's baby son lived for only 14 months. Like many, Mick hadn't dealt with the loss. Like me, he thought he could keep moving, drinking and partying so the pain wouldn't have a place to land. I've since learned that this is a particularly common coping mechanism when headstrong, active people face loss. Mick was always his own person, an independent, freewheeling party animal. Although that free quality was what I most admired about him, at the same time, I found it hard to accept that Mick wasn't always available. Grief was still raw inside me and I needed someone to cling to. I needed a rock for my emotions to crash against, but Mick was a rolling stone at heart and I knew he was not looking to gather any moss. I worried constantly that I would lose what we had together.

I was 21 years old and up to now, life had been hellish, to say the least. But I was a survivor and I was determined to make the most of life from now on. Mick and I enjoyed the biker lifestyle and went to a bike rally over the last weekend of May. Staying overnight with friends, Crystal had had great fun visiting a local fete and having her face painted. Things weren't ideal, but there was still room for optimism. I had a new man, a daughter I loved and the future was looking good. I tried to let the unanswered questions about Martin's death fade into the past and to keep things as friendly as possible with Tony. I tried hard not to cling too hard to Mick. Most of all, I was so grateful for my little Crystal and her soothing, unconditional love. No matter what happened, I knew we would always be there for each other.

On June 6, Crystal's grandparents came to pick her up for her month-long visit with Tony. Although I enjoyed the freedom from responsibility that these visits gave me, I was already beginning to miss her as I packed her bags and got her ready. She was all dressed up when her grandparents arrived, with her hair in pigtails (her favourite hairstyle at the time). Her grandparents had brought her Cabbage Patch doll with them, which ironically had pigtails and even looked a little like her. I stood at the front door as they drove away and my mind took a photo of my daughter waving goodbye with the doll in her arms. I watched the car for as long as I could see it, with my daughter still waving goodbye. I have never forgotten that moment.

* * *

Ten days later, on June 16th, I turned 22. On the night of the 26th, I had a dream. It was one of the most real dreams I have ever had and I still remember it in detail:

I was with Mick and another friend who was holding a baby. Somehow, I knew the baby belonged to us all. I was holding Crystal's hand. We walked through an archway into a grassy foyer and then through another archway. There were people everywhere. The ground sloped upwards and everyone was walking up the incline. They all looked like they were sleepwalking, even my friend and my partner. Suddenly, I felt Crystal disappear.

Immediately frantic, I tore back the way we had come to try find her.

"Have you seen a little girl, about this high, with sandy brown hair?" I begged a passer by. He just shook his head. I went back through the second archway and saw a hippy we had passed earlier. Stopping in front of him sitting on the ground, I repeated the same question:

"Have you seen a little girl with sandy brown hair - about this high?"

"No man," he answered solemnly, "she's gone." Distressed, I pleaded with him, "You must remember. We just passed by with her!"

The hippy just looked me in the eyes. "No man, she's gone," he said.

When I awoke from that dream, I ran into Crystal's bedroom, heart pounding and dripping with sweat. I was freaking out. For several seconds, I stared at my daughter's untouched bed in a state of panic before I registered that she was still at her father's. Breathing a huge sigh of relief, I went back to bed but was still uneasy because the dream had seemed so real. The next day, Friday, the dream lingered in my thoughts. At lunchtime, Mick and I were searching for a new puppy we had taken to a friend's place. We hunted high and low for about two hours, finally finding the little dog curled up for a sleep in a quiet spot. I remember telling Mick that I thought my dream must somehow have been related to the hunt for the lost puppy.

The uneasiness wouldn't go away though.

That night, I made my usual phone call to my daughter. For the first time in the two years she had been visiting her father, Crystal was upset and wanted to come home. She was crying and begging me to pick her up. She said she wanted me to drive the six hours and come and get her right away. I tried to calm her down, but couldn't console her. Apparently, her father had been working away and Crystal was only seeing him on the weekends. This bothered me greatly, but there was not much I could do except try to cheer her up. After all, I reassured her, it was only a few more sleeps until she would be back in her own bed. Besides, there would be a lovely surprise waiting for her when she got home. Mick and I were going to buy her a swing-set the following Sunday. I didn't go into details – it would spoil the surprise. Crystal was inconsolable. I had never had to deal with this before and it was very upsetting for both of us. Ending the conversation with a very heavy heart, I called my mother and related the conversation to her. Mum also intended to call Crystal that night but decided against it because she didn't want to hear her so upset. We both agreed that it would be great to have her home the following week.

The 28th of June 1986 began like many other Saturdays for me. Mick was going to a 'biker bash' and I was going out with my girlfriends to a party. We planned to meet up later in the evening. One of my friends was having a huge fight with her bloke about the biker bash and was generally a pain in the butt all night. At about 8.30pm, my friend Hope and I decided to take her home. Something didn't feel right. I was uneasy and she was angry and bitter. After we dropped her off, Hope and I decided to go to the beach and finish off our drinks. We had been friends since we were 11, and on that night we talked in depth about our lives. Most of all, we talked about my dead brother who had the same birthday as Hope's. We laughed and cried and reminisced late into the night. Despite the large amount of alcohol I had consumed, I still felt as clear as a bell when I got home. I had slept for about two hours when Mick called me from the party I had been at earlier and asked me to pick him up. So I went and found him (after much searching - he was a wild man) and we finally went home and fell asleep. We both needed it - we were going on a ride to the coast with our friends in the morning.

* * *

Sunday morning, 6 a.m. A loud banging at the door wakes me. I race out of the bedroom, alarmed to see a uniformed police officer standing on the doorstep. My mind races at a million miles an hour: Did I pay that speeding fine? Yes. Had Mick got himself into some sort of trouble? What was wrong? I open the door.

"Are you Mrs Charmaine Wilson?" asks the police-man.

I nod, panic welling inside the confusion.

"Do you have a daughter, Crystal Wilson?"

"Yes - why?" The minute I ask that question, I wish I could take it back.

The policeman tells me he is here to inform me that Crystal has been fatally injured in a car accident.

I feel the panic begin to bubble over, but my mind is not registering the meaning of his words. What?? What does he mean, 'fatally injured'? Has she lost an arm or leg? What is wrong - what kind of injuries? What does 'fatally injured' mean? My head spins. The word 'fatally' just won't - can't - mustn't - compute in my brain. I ask him to repeat himself.

The policeman tries to calm me down, asking if I have anyone with me, to which I reply 'yes'. Mick comes out to see what's happening. I feel hysteria bursting out of me and into the room. The police officer backs away, visibly upset.

I still can't figure it out. What is wrong? Why won't anyone answer me?

I call Crystal's grandfather in New South Wales – he will be able to tell me what's going on – he will be able to tell me what's happened to my daughter.

"What is wrong with Crystal? Has she lost an arm or leg? What is wrong?" I beg, gripping the phone receiver like a lifeline and willing an answer that will wake me up from this nightmare.

The voice on the other end of the phone says, "Crystal is dead."

I drop the phone and scream.

Chapter 3

Black Oceans

I think Mick picked up the telephone and spoke to Crystal's grandfather. I can't be sure - all I could hear was my own screaming. Tragedy had returned and this time the shockwave was a million times more powerful. The hole inside my heart ripped wide open, the pain in my chest so intense I couldn't breathe. It felt like I had lost orbit in space and was floating around an empty universe with nothing to hold onto. From my position in distant space, I could still hear someone screaming. It was me. Panic took over along with denial as I struggled to absorb what was going on around me.

I had to fix it. They were wrong. It could be fixed. They had the wrong Crystal. They must have. My daughter was alive and we were going to buy her a swing-set the next day. She was coming home next week. I grabbed a cigarette and smoked it quickly. I called my mother. I cried the news down the phone to her. She told me later on that she thought I was having a fight with Mick. She came over with my stepfather and we all cried. For the first time in my life, I smoked in front of my mother - cigarette after cigarette. The boys came to pick us up for the bike ride. I wanted to go – in fact, I got hysterical and insisted that we go. After all, I reasoned, there was nothing we could do, was there? Crystal was dead. Now let's just move on and go for a ride! I clawed at any opportunity to escape this room, these feelings, this reality.

The tears would not stop flowing. Apart from the most vivid moments, that day remains a blur. As do the days immediately following. I just drank and smoked. I was not walking around in a fog this time as I had been when Martin died. This time, the breakers weren't knocking me off my feet. No, this time I was wading through thick blackness at the bottom of the ocean where no one could help me. I was suffocating and dying but no one could save me. I was not a mother anymore but my womb screamed otherwise. And the flow of questions matched the flow of tears. Where was my baby? Where was she? Martin must have come to get her. Why couldn't he leave her here? No, No! This was a mistake. They would all see this when we went to the funeral. It would not be Crystal in the coffin. They had made a mistake. No, no, no!

The funeral was to be held in New South Wales as we could not afford to transport Crystal's body back to Queensland. We made the sad trek down there on July 1st. I remember buying two white roses, one for Crystal and one for her grandmother, Pam. One rose began to wilt almost immediately. I wanted Mick to confirm my suspicions that they had made a mistake. He tried to help me accept the truth, telling me there was no mistake. I hated him at that moment for siding with 'them'. We arrived in Kempsey and got a room for the night. My mother gave me a sedative to help me sleep. It seemed like I would never be able to sleep again, but I must have.

The next morning was beautiful. July 2nd, my grandmother's birthday. We drove to Crystal's grandparents' place first. No one had to point out to me where the accident had occurred. I felt icy, icy cold as we passed the site. The accident had happened at 8.30pm on

June 28th. Tony had been drinking at a barbeque and lost control of the car on a straight stretch of road on the way home. He broke his leg, had his spleen removed and was now in hospital. My daughter, Crystal, suffocated on her tongue and died quickly. There were no broken bones, no other injuries - just a few bruises. No one witnessed the accident. Although you could see the accident site from their back door, Tony's parents didn't hear a thing until the ambulances came. As we walked into the house, Deep Purple's *Child in Time* was playing on the record player. I don't hear that song often these days, but when I do, it catapults me straight back to that day - straight back to that very minute, right into the pain.

The funeral was to be held at the Uniting Church in Kempsey and then Crystal was to be cremated. Martin had been cremated and his ashes thrown on the water at his favourite fishing spot. Most of the people who actually knew Crystal were not able to attend because of the distance and of course the short notice. My idea was that if we had her cremated, we could have another ceremony in Brisbane. Before we left Brisbane, we made the decision to view Crystal's body. I, for one, needed proof that my daughter was really gone. Martin had appeared so peaceful - surely it couldn't be all bad – it might even help if I could just say goodbye. Of course, somewhere inside me I still believed I would look at the child in the coffin and realise they had the wrong person.

The minister who was holding the ceremony wished to speak to me before the viewing to see if there was anything I wanted said at the service. I handed him this poem I had written:

Pure as the whitest rose
Touched with innocence
She filled our lives with happiness
So it doesn't make much sense
Why one so young, innocent and pure
Couldn't live some more
Why was she taken from our lives
When she was only four?
This is to Crystal Charee
Our White Rose
In The Garden of Thorns

Well, here came my first shock for the day. The minister flatly refused to read the poem, arguing that life was not a 'garden of thorns'. I replied that it certainly looked that way to me right now. Nevertheless, he handed it back to me, refusing to read it at the service. I was still reeling from his insensitivity as Mick led me to the private viewing room to see my daughter.

When I think back on all the painful moments of my life, I would have to say that the moment I saw my four-year-old daughter lying in a coffin would have to be on top of the list. There she was, the little girl who just a few short weeks before was smiling and waving goodbye with pigtails and a Cabbage Patch doll to match. She was not smiling now. She looked sad and one of her eyes was partially open. There was a bruise on the right side of her forehead. Surreally, I wondered how she had got it. She was wearing a pink dress that looked too young for her and had a gold chain around her neck. She was in the full sunlight, which I suppose made her look worse. She did not look peaceful - she looked dead. And so sad. My heart exploded.

I moved to the side of the coffin and picked up her little hand. There was the nail polish still on her fingers that mum had put on the week or so before she left. Chipped and worn, but now her fingers were bruised. I felt the front of her dress, there was padding there and my mind went into overdrive thinking about the autopsy. I picked her up and tried to shake her alive, repeating over and over, "Wake up, please wake up." In the end, I had to be forcibly removed from the room. Many years have passed since that day, but every tiny detail of that viewing is as vivid to me now as it was then. I can still close my eyes and see that scene as clearly as if I had just walked into the room. I have never viewed a body since that day, though God knows I have had opportunities. In my heart, I do not feel I will ever put myself through that again.

The funeral was terrible. There was no poem, no mention of Crystal at all except for "Crystal was a nice little girl who we all loved very much". It was a stock standard, fill-in-the-blanks Christian funeral service, with quote after quote from the Bible to pad out the time. All the while, the coffin was there. It was white and small and my baby was inside it. Mick and my mum had to stop me from leaving. I felt physically and mentally sick throughout the whole impersonal, hypocritical fiasco. By the time the service was over and we all went outside, I had just stopped feeling and was literally trying to go back a week in time. I looked up and saw my friends, Scotty and Tarina, who had cut work for the day to be with me. They were like a rainbow on a very black day. I just held onto Scotty and cried and cried. We went to a pub and started drinking.

I didn't stop drinking for 16 years.

* * *

On the way back to Brisbane, we spent a few days in the mountains of Nimbin with Marcus, a friend of Mick's. Marcus looked very much like the hippy in my dream. Temporarily away from all that was familiar, and thanks to a constant supply of guava wine and sedatives, I was able to get a bit of distance from reality. And where better than Nimbin for that to happen? I'd always heard Nimbin was a magical place, so it's not surprising that strange things happened there right after Crystal's death.

On our first day there, I had my back to the door when Mick told me to turn around slowly. He had seen Crystal standing at the door looking in. The following day, a woman came to visit Marcus with her two-year-old nephew. It was strange as he was the first child I had seen since the accident. He came straight over to me, sat on my lap and gave me the biggest cuddle. Then he sat back and looked into the darkened room. He turned and said to me, "Who is that little girl in there? Why won't she come out and play?" My heart froze, but try as I might I could not see Crystal though I am sure that's who the little boy could see. She was following me. Marcus had no phone, no power and in the hills of Nimbin, people drop by without notice. His girlfriend could not have known we were there, let alone anything of our predicament. The little boy was just telling me what he saw. As for Mick, trust me when I say Mick is a diehard sceptic. Yet, to this day, he still tells people about seeing Crystal with his own eyes in that doorway at Nimbin.

* * *

When we got home, I had a burning desire to have a 'proper' ceremony for Crystal in Brisbane. I wanted to have her ashes taken to Mount Tamborine and spread at the same place as Mick had spread his baby son's ashes years before. I began making phone enquiries as to when I might receive the ashes. My idea was to wait until Tony was well and have the ceremony with him. He had been unable to attend the funeral due to his injuries. The funeral director informed me that the ashes could not be released to me as Tony's parents had signed 'the body' in. I called his mother who flatly refused to discuss the topic. I rang Tony who called me some names and hung up in my ear. I phoned the funeral director again. This time he bluntly stated that there was no way 'anyone like me' could have the ashes. Apparently he had heard all about me and was not prepared to negotiate. I was going insane – I just couldn't understand where all the animosity was coming from. All that I wanted was to have her near. Tony refused to talk to me. He was undergoing psychiatric treatment.

As a last resort I contacted a solicitor. She took immediate steps to have the ashes withheld, meaning no one could spread them until all parties were co-operating. She let Tony's solicitor know on the Friday that a court order would be presented the following Monday, preventing his family from spreading the ashes. So quite simply, they spread them on the Sunday! It rocked my whole existence that people could be so cruel. I had no intention of spreading the ashes before Tony was ready, nor did I wish to halve them as had been suggested. In fact, the thought never entered my mind. I know Tony was not in his right mind – he was beside himself with guilt and grief. But how could anyone even think I intended to do that? They just spread the ashes over the Kempsey cemetery, put up a plaque and my daughter became a memory. Just like that, in the course of a weekend, the decision had been taken from my hands. To this day, I still cannot believe I was left out of a ceremony so important for closure. Over time we can forgive the hurtful things people do, especially under extremely tragic circumstances. In all honesty though, I do not think I will ever understand or accept the reasons I was given for my daughter's ashes to be scattered without my presence or consent. I was young, distraught with grief and desperate to do this last thing for her. This had been my last request as a mother. It was completely devastating.

Tony was sent to jail for culpable driving and driving whilst under the influence of alcohol. He was out after six months.

* * *

Those were black days. They turned into black weeks and black months. It was like existing in a nightmare from which it was impossible to escape. I desperately wanted to wake up but didn't know how. I was not a mother anymore but still felt like one. My head would echo with memories and then the guilt would come crushing down. There were a lot of questions and 'if-onlys' after Martin's death, but that was nothing in comparison. The rollercoaster ride was higher, faster and filled with agonising loops. I was tearing myself apart with every second of every day, over-analysing Crystal's entire life. Every harsh word, every refusal, every missed opportunity replayed in my mind like a never-ending movie. I blamed myself cruelly for everything I had ever done or not done as a parent. I should have done this and why didn't I do that? Was I a good enough mother? I didn't think so. If I had known she would be leaving so soon, I would never have chastised her, never have wasted a second of our precious time together. On and on it went: the guilt, the anger at my inexperience, the pain of remembering, the fear of forgetting any tiny detail. Once again, I had questions, so many questions. Once again, there were no answers, so I just grieved.

I ordered a pack of tarot cards through my book club. I was trying to find Crystal but the cards didn't reveal anything that comforted or helped me. I must have done about half a dozen readings before I put them away. In retrospect, all of the readings were very accurate but I just wasn't ready to receive the information. All I wanted was to make contact with my daughter or with someone or something who could tell me she was ok where she was.

I only have a few clear memories of the first six months after Crystal left and I now understand that I was in shock. This is a common symptom after the death of a child. The pain was just unbearable. I tried to fill the enormous burning hole in my heart with alcohol but it didn't change the fact that life could never be the same after what had happened. I knew I was now a different person. It wasn't possible to hang on to who I was before, but letting go was very, very hard. My mind could not find a soft place to land. The past was a minefield of memories, the present just unbearable and I couldn't imagine any kind of future without my daughter. I didn't know who I was anymore, and mostly, I didn't care. Six months after the funeral, I was drinking very heavily which usually led to massive arguments with Mick. I would get drunk and morbid and would just cry and cry. What was going through Mick's head, I can't even imagine. He'd been through the death of a child before and it must have opened up a Pandora's box of emotions for him, but I was too deep inside my own grief to notice or to care.

I was coping the only way I knew, but it was hard for the people who loved me to stand by and watch me destroying myself. Grandpop was terribly upset that I couldn't seem to snap back. People began avoiding me because they didn't know what to say about Crystal. Sometimes they did say the wrong things, sometimes they were a great comfort. Friends just dropped out of my life when I needed them most and that hurt. To this day, I still haven't seen some of the people I considered good friends back then. The friends who did stick around didn't have a clue what to do for me. I had lost my brother, my daughter and now many of my friends as well. Most difficult of all, I had lost myself - and I didn't have a clue where to start looking.

* * *

Although the pain I felt inside was relentless, almost imperceptibly over time the darkness started to lift. Instead of asking questions, I began to seek answers. As each day passed, I felt myself swimming slowly from the depth of the seabed towards the surface of the ocean. I was still holding my breath, my lungs aching with the effort, but for the first time in ages, I felt like I might reach the air if I just kept swimming hard enough. So I took my first steps back out into the world by enrolling in a community childcare course. I threw myself into studying and received the highest ever recorded score at the time. It was not a major course but it gave me comfort to feel that I was achieving something. The teacher tried to encourage me to go further, so I volunteered my time at a nearby childcare centre. By this time, I had been off work for six months and needed to earn some money if I was going to begin picking up the pieces of my life again.

On the day my daughter was supposed to start school, I started work at a local factory, packing cooked chicken pieces into boxes. I was very upset that day, more so than usual because it was a 'milestone day' that Crystal and I wouldn't be able to share. The lady across from me on the production line introduced herself as Collette. She had four children, was happily married and worked night shift while her husband looked after the kids. He worked days. She was a very slim woman with a heap of energy and she talked me through that first day comforting me repeatedly. I was crying tears all over the chicken and Collette's soothing words helped me very much. Although we didn't become close friends, Collette always stopped me to say hello and I was always pleased to see her. She had begun working in a different section so we didn't get to talk as often as we would have liked. Three months after I started working at the factory, I went to work and everyone was upset or crying. Collette and her husband had been killed outright in a car accident on the previous Friday evening. Four kids were left without parents and here I was, a mother without any kids. I walked out of the factory and never went back. This world was all wrong and if there was a God, well, he needed to be sacked!

Not long afterwards, on the 20th of September 1987, Grandpop, the man who had always been able to make me laugh, passed away at the Greenslopes veterans' hospital. Up until the time Crystal died, I used to go and clean his caravan. I'd help him boil up his giant vats of tomato relish made with bargain boxes of tomatoes. After Crystal died, I didn't want to clean Grandpop's caravan anymore. I didn't want to live. Neither did Grandpop after that. I always felt he died of a broken heart because his great grandchild and grandchild had preceded him. He had battled with lung disease his whole life but gave up the fight then − I think he 'pointed the bone' at himself. The last time I spoke to him, we both cried. I asked him to say hello to Martin and Crystal for me when he got to heaven. I wish I had said something else - that I loved him - but I didn't. My grandfather had served in World War II and because of this, *The Last Post* was played at his funeral. The tears flowed and although I accepted his death a lot easier than the others, I still miss him and think of him often. He really was a great character.

Chapter 4

Chasing the Aussie Dream

I wandered the earth like a grey zombie for a long time. And then one day, it hit me: I needed to get myself a suntan! I know that must sound strange, but I had become obsessed with my skin colour. I don't like to lie out in the hot sun, so I found a tanning bed at the local gym and spent many hours browning myself to perfection. Each day as I walked out, I would pass the aerobics room. In 1987, aerobics was a new rage. It fascinated me to watch the classes. All my dreams of dance came to the surface. I remembered a year earlier how much fun Crystal, my friend Dot and I had working out to an exercise video. I took the plunge. Dressed in pink leotard and tights I had purchased at a Lifeline charity shop, I walked in and joined up classes for a month. That day as I left the class feeling somewhat exhausted, I felt something give. At last, I knew I had found an outlet for all the anger and grief pent up inside me. I did not miss a single aerobics class during that first month nor in the next three months after that. I enjoyed it so much, I enrolled to become an aerobics instructor myself.

As I had done with the childcare course, I threw myself into instructor training. By 1988, I was a qualified aerobics instructor, popular with my classes and involved in competitions. My life was back on track and had been for a while. Mick and I still drank heavily on weekends and continued to argue a lot but hey, that was the *Australian Way*, wasn't it? At 24 and 30, Mick and I had lost two children between us so when I discovered I was pregnant, we were both over the moon. I was about to qualify as a 'Fitness Leader' and had been very excited about it, but that would have to wait for now. We were so excited about the arrival of our new baby – it signalled the beginning of a fresh chapter in our lives together. Mick treated me like a queen throughout my whole pregnancy. We couldn't wait for the birth.

Our son, Alan John, was born on the 10th of February 1989. It wasn't an easy delivery - our eagerly-awaited new arrival weighed over nine pounds and the birth process was long, complicated and stressful. Without going into the gory details, let's just say that mummy couldn't sit for a very long time after the birth. The baby had some lung problems that required a short sunbake in an incubator at the premmy ward. How strange it was to see our big 9lb 5oz bruiser in a room with all the tiny premmies!

Alan was a calm baby, easy to feed and a good sleeper right from the start. His Dad, on the other hand, was not quite so well-behaved. On the day of the birth, Mick went out to celebrate in the tradition of so many Aussie men before him - by 'getting pissed' with his mates. Feeling ten feet tall and bullet-proof after siring a nine-pound male heir, Mick decided to give a friend's British motorbike a test run. In his celebratory 'pissed-ness', he overlooked the fact that on British bikes, the controls work in the opposite way. He accelerated with unmatched skill - straight into a brick wall!

I was still in my hospital bed, very sore and very worried about Alan lying in his humidicrib. When they came to tell me about Mick's accident, the room began to swirl around me and I felt my world come crashing in all over again. I thought Mick was dead. Life was just too cruel – how could this happen to me over and over again?

I eventually calmed down enough to register the news that Mick was alive but had sustained serious injuries including a broken arm, leg and other bones. At that point, I entertained thoughts of killing him myself! To make matters worse, Mick was in the 'biker ward' in a hospital on the other side of town. I had trouble walking with my birthing injuries and I still couldn't sit, but I managed to struggle my way from one hospital to the other, life-preserver shaped cushion in hand, to visit my dashing biker-prince in his hospital bed. He was lying still, covered in external fixations like a giant pincushion. It was a frightening sight.

"Oh, my God," my poor hero whispered, his face filled with obvious pain. "You have tits – and I can't even touch 'em!"

I didn't know whether to smooch him or inflict a few fresh injuries of my own.

Alan came home from hospital after a week. Mick was in a wheelchair for six months and out of action for twelve. It felt like I had two babies to look after. It was a very trying and stressful time, so I returned to the gym to work out my frustrations and get my body back in shape. I began working as a Fitness Instructor when Alan was about three months old. I got seriously fit and became very involved in the gym scene. I entered an aerobics instructor competition and came second. Meanwhile,

Mick was incredibly frustrated - he didn't take to having his wings clipped and naturally took his frustrations out on the closest person - me. I understood where it was coming from but I was barely keeping my own head above water with work, training and the new baby. Things became very tense between us. In 1992, I trained as a bodybuilder for the first time. I would train at the gym for up to four hours a day. After three months, I came fourth in a women's bodybuilding competition. Exercise was a bit of an addiction for me – like anything I became obsessed with, I just couldn't stop. Mostly, those were good times but secretly I was disappointed that things hadn't changed much at home. Bringing our new baby home had not transformed us into the Brady Bunch at all. I felt like Alice the housekeeper most of the time. Well, Alice with a fantastic body anyway!

* * *

Five years after Alan was born, we bought a block of land at Stanthorpe near where my mother lived. My daughter had been gone for eight years and I still missed her terribly, but life was looking up and despite the fighting, it seemed Mick and I were making some real progress at last. Stanthorpe is a beautiful place in Queensland's southern Granite Belt, renowned for its stone-fruit and cold winters. As a builder, Mick had big dreams for that block. I was pregnant again at 30 and despite nine years as an aerobics instructor on and off, this pregnancy was harder. I was older and I was tired. I watched helplessly from the sidelines as Mick succumbed to another well-known syndrome affecting many Australian men - the

Wild Colonial Boy's obsession with building his dream castle with his bare hands on his own patch of ground. As 'Constructor' toiled like a demon, measuring, hammering, sawing and making a lot of grunting sounds and power tool noise, I just wanted to lie on the couch and watch my belly grow. The cracks began to appear in our relationship.

Stanthorpe, like many rural or semi-rural areas, is a bit of a 'closed shop'. It's a place where you don't become a local just by having a local address. The trust and friendship of the community has to be earned, and acceptance comes over time as you become involved in local customs and get to know the locals on their terms. The only time I saw the neighbours during the early part of our time there was when someone's cow got lost on our property. It was a lonely pregnancy for me, and Mick couldn't understand why I wasn't as enthusiastic or as helpful as he wanted me to be. I just couldn't find it in me. At 32 weeks, I began to bleed.

The doctors had difficulty figuring out what the problem was, so I was kept under careful observation in hospital for the five weeks leading up to Jack's birth. This confinement didn't do much to alleviate the boredom and loneliness I was feeling, even though the sounds of labouring women kept me awake day and night. All I had to look forward to each day was the hospital food. I came to know the daily menu by heart - and my weight ballooned. To keep occupied, I wheeled myself around (between meals) and conducted the 'Ring Test' on expectant mums to determine the sex of their babies. This test is as old as the hills and has been practiced by wise women for many centuries. A piece of string is tied to the pregnant woman's wedding ring which is held suspended in midair. The string is held very still and eventually, it moves by itself in one direction or another. The movement of the ring determines the sex of the new arrival. For my test, if it moved around in circles, it meant a girl was on the way. If it swung back and forth, it would be a boy. During my five weeks at the prenatal ward, I had a 100% accuracy rate and became a bit of a celebrity with the nurses and mums. It didn't occur to me that this might have been more than just a series of lucky guesses on my part. I just wanted to have my baby and go home.

Alan was now five years old and missing me badly. My relationship with Mick had soured rapidly at Stanthorpe and I was concerned Mick's open animosity towards me would affect Alan the longer I was away. I asked the doctors to bring Jack on early - I just couldn't bear the waiting any longer. So, our beautiful second son was born on the 19th of July 1994. Clearly unimpressed that he had to enter this world before he was ready, Jack was not a calm baby. I nicknamed him 'Screamin' Jack. He vacuumed half my nipple off during his first feed and screamed the hospital down, but I couldn't help admiring his strength and determination. Jack had entered the building and he wanted the world to know all about it! When I walked back through the door at Stanthorpe, many kilos heavier, depressed, miserable and with a very vocal new baby to add to the mix, the reception from Mick was less than warm. Alan wasn't even talking to me. I knew the odds were stacked against us as never before.

Mick's attitude towards me worsened dramatically in the weeks that followed. His talent for making me feel beautiful and sexy was devastatingly effective in reverse. I felt like the most undesirable goblin on earth and to be honest, I could have won an Oscar for the role. As my self-esteem plummeted, it's no surprise that our fighting increased. We had always been drinkers, but before long we were drinking separately and heavier than ever. Escaping his 'squawking kid and fat wife' at every opportunity, Mick disappeared to 'drink with the neighbours' for days at a time. Before long, I had enough of sitting around staring at the walls. I needed to spend time with friendly people over the age of five, or I felt I would completely lose my mind. With mum nearby to look after the children, it was time for me to go back to work. In a stroke of alcohol-fuelled brilliance, I got myself a job at the local pub.

I was immediately in my element. The drunks at the hotel were always quick to tell me how gorgeous I was and my ego was listening to every word they said. At last, I had met the locals! Alhough I could feel my confidence slowly returning, the patterns of fighting and separate partying continued. I decided I couldn't stay with Mick. Around this time, I met Pedro. He was young and beautiful, with the greenest eyes I've ever seen. Pedro spoke as though the future of the planet hinged on my happiness. He reminded me of my worth as a person and tried to help me stop drinking. Pedro nurtured me and helped me to disentangle myself from the mess that my life with Mick had become. I took the plunge and moved with the kids to a house about ten kilometres away.

My job at the pub kept me sane through that period – once again I was able to distract myself from my problems by keeping busy and working hard. I worked as upstairs and downstairs maid in all the bars and in the bottle-shop, learning everything I could about running a hotel. It was a great little country pub and in spite of all that was going on at the time, I have many great memories of working there. Eventually, as sweet as Pedro was, when Mick gave up drinking and asked me back, I didn't hesitate to go home. Within two hours of my return, I knew I had made a mistake - the trust between us was clearly damaged beyond repair. To give Mick his due, he did try to help me quit the booze, but living together only perpetuated long-established destructive patterns we had both lived with for too long. I stayed with Mick for six months and in 1997, we split for the last time. Some time later, I heard that sweet, gentle Pedro had died of a drug overdose. I guess, like many giving souls in this world, Pedro didn't think it was important to nurture himself.

Chapter 5

Stonefruit: Toxic Times

During the harvest season, Stanthorpe fills with itinerant fruit pickers from across Australia and the world. I would occasionally work on local farms during the season. It was a great way to exercise and meet amazing people from all walks of life. During one harvest season after separating from Mick, I met Nigel. Nigel was the boyfriend every girl with addiction problems dreams of. Where Pedro and Mick had tried to stop my drinking, Nigel encouraged me. Being with him was liberating - he accepted me for who I was – he didn't feel the burning desire to rescue me from myself like everyone else did.

Mick had the boys two nights a week, Tuesdays and Saturdays. On those nights, Nigel and I would get together with a group of musicians and have jam sessions. With the kids safely out of harm's way, I would let myself go. Alcohol, marijuana and various other kinds of drugs flowed freely, a lot of them into my bloodstream. I felt wild and beautiful, like a gypsy dancer by an open fire. I was living 'The Musician's Life' – the life of a free creative spirit, living in the moment. Or so I told myself. Deep down, I knew I was just following a long-established pattern - blotting out my pain, convincing myself I was having fun as I drank my life down the drain.

I was thrilled when my old school friend Hope announced she was coming to stay with me. Now I would have someone else to share the antics with, someone else besides Nigel who wouldn't judge me. I thought about our friendship. Through all the adolescent highs and lows, my teenage pregnancy, marriage saga and all the heartbreak and loss that had followed, Hope was always Hope. When my family were being impossible and didn't understand me, she encouraged me to ignore them and have fun. When I was falling apart over losing Martin and later Crystal, Hope had pointed out that tragic death was simply a reminder that life was short and that we shouldn't waste time thinking about consequences, but live in the moment. No matter what state I was in, she was always the same, full of inspired scams that allowed us to get away with just about anything right under the noses of any authority that stood in our way. Hope lived by her own rules and didn't seem to suffer over hurts for long – nothing seemed to stop her from pursuing what she wanted. She had a knack for popping up at the most painful and difficult times of my life and making everything seem like an adventure.

I had always adored Hope because she walked the talk. What you saw was what you got. She didn't give a shit about consequences or what anyone else thought, whereas I knew I was a fraud. On the surface I was having a ball - jam sessions, partying and squeezing every drop out of life. But the truth was I was incredibly vulnerable and broken-hearted, ashamed of my choices and rapidly losing control of my life because of my addiction to alcohol. Inside, I felt the old self-loathing stronger than ever. I knew I was a bad mother, a bad wife, a rotten person. When Hope came to stay, I felt safer. She was stronger than me, much harder and less broken. If I stuck with her and followed her lead, then I knew everything would turn out ok. Hope knew how to navigate through life without sustaining serious injuries.

We are responsible for our own choices in life but I do believe it is very important to be aware of the company we attract, especially at times when we are desperate or grieving. Don't get me wrong here: I'm not suggesting that we can blame another person for our problems, but the environment that individual friendships thrive in is an important clue to whether that friendship is healthy or not. As far as Hope was concerned, this was a lesson I had to learn the hard way. At one of the toughest times of my life, Hope re-entered my world. I trusted her and depended on her to care about what happened to me and my children. I handed my power to her without hesitation. I didn't know at the time that Hope had a serious addiction to amphetamines (or speed, as it's commonly called). Not that it would have mattered if I had known, really. I loved her and accepted that she was a 'naughty girl' from way back. I trusted her as someone who could handle herself in the long run. I believed she would always watch my back. I couldn't have been more wrong.

When I walked into Hope's room one night and caught her self-administering amphetamines, it took me completely by surprise. Unfortunately, I was also instantly intrigued. My inner voice was screaming at me to walk away, but of course I ignored it. After all, Hope was still Hope – she didn't seem to be caught up in any kind of chemical nightmare. Perhaps all the bad things I had heard about speed addiction were wrong. Perhaps I could just try it and see for myself…

"Are you sure?" Hope asked almost casually, hardly taking her eyes from the task at hand. Of course, I had no reservations about taking lessons in drug use from my trusted friend of twenty years. After all, Hope always knew what she was doing and never got herself into a scrape she couldn't get out of. In one of those unguarded moments that we live to regret, the reckless gypsy in me danced straight into the campfire…

As I said, I don't blame anyone for the choices I have made in my life. I don't hold Hope responsible for the decision I made that night. But having said that, and having been through the hell of amphetamine addiction myself, I now understand that a true friend would have at least tried to discourage my curiosity at that moment. Anyone who believes the old wives' tale that you can't get addicted over 20, is kidding themselves. I truly believed I could control drugs rather than letting them control me. I believed Hope when she assured me it was possible. Wrong again. Speed takes you down very fast and before long, I would find myself spiraling towards a new kind of darkness that held me in its grip for almost three years. As I jumped headfirst into a very serious battle for my life, Hope set about taking me for everything I had.

It didn't occur to me back then that a friend who always turns up when you find yourself at rock-bottom, doesn't necessarily have your best interest at heart. There's a particular kind of friend who circles in the sky above until all support systems are gone. The last emotional valuables are left unguarded and nothing but pain clings to our bones. It takes some hard experience to realise that this kind of friend comes down to land at such times not to offer a lifeline, but to feast on the carcass. It's a very painful lesson to learn – one that brings all prior notions of trust into question.

Fortunately, if we survive the experience, these friends teach us the simplest and most valuable lesson of all: The person ultimately responsible for protecting yourself from your own bad choices is You. Therefore, the most important friendship to develop in life must be the one with yourself.

For many of us, the process of listening to our own inner guidance takes some getting used to. Not all of us are lucky enough to have childhoods that give us the tools to navigate through life wisely or even safely. Sometimes we do, but life's lessons have taught us not to trust our instincts. If we can find the friend inside ourselves – the one that thinks about consequences and demands we take care of our own health and wellbeing no matter what situations we are faced with - that friend will never let us down. Many years on and after much ill-health and heartache, I have learned to listen to that inner voice. Hope is no longer in my life, but I thank her for teaching me that lesson.

* * *

As my toxic honeymoon with Nigel, Hope, alcohol and drugs continued, things began to deteriorate at every level. My father died that February and I was struggling with a new form of escape that was increasingly impossible to resist:

The Addiction

Time ticks on, suffocating heat
Sweat from your pores, smells of defeat
Nightmares so bad you just can't retreat
Release so close, so, so sweet

Walls close in ,bending your brain
The madness starts, you're going insane
Let your mind unbend, don't refrain
See the rainbows, won't you smile again

Cool relief it's quick and fast
The pain subsides, the tension is past
Your mind takes off with a roaring blast
Body and soul together at last.

I'm in you now, no turning back
I give you pleasure I don't lack
I give you pain, my heart is black
Are you tripped out by society
Break the chains, I'll set you free
Racing, chasing run with glee
Its too late now, you're running with me

Come on down, all things must end
You're mind was mind only on lend
Into society you must blend
Until we meet and you're needs I tend.

After Dad died, I had a dream:

I picked Dad up in the red car that he'd bought me. As I drove along, he turned to me and asked, "Do you know where you're going?"

"Yep, yeah" I said, "we turn just up here." Dad looked at me and nodded and I turned the car right, then right again. We came to a park and ahead lay a cliff, and each side of the cliff just dropped into nothing.

"Stop right there - don't go any further," Dad warned.

"OK," I said and stopped the car.

I got Dad's wheelchair out of the car and pushed him across a narrow reach up to a house. I could see our family inside and raced in to greet them.

"Is he here yet?" the family members asked me eagerly, as Dad wheeled himself inside the room.

"Dad," I waved him over, "it's so-and-so. He wants to know if you're home yet." Dad looked at me with the most radiant smile of his life – I'll never forget it – and he said, "Yep, I'm home!"

Dad's third wife, Helen, was there. I had to go to the chemist. Helen said her car was in the way and she went to move it. But she drove straight forward, and I followed her. The next thing I knew, the whole car was falling apart. I was just hanging on to a mudguard and I was falling, falling, falling....

* * *

Mick moved to South Australia during this time, to live with his new girlfriend. In July of '99, he came back to Stanthorpe to see the boys and took them to visit his family for the weekend. My car had blown up in Brisbane a few weeks before and I had been stuck without transport for a while until I could find a way to get the car back to Stanthorpe. The car was still under repair when Mick arrived. He arranged to drop the boys back at my mother's house on the following Monday. Taking advantage of the time off, I hopped on a bus and went to visit friends for the weekend. When I arrived back in Stanthorpe, I called home for my mother to come and pick me up from the bus station. Once again, my stepfather broke the bad news. Mick had taken the boys. They were now thousands of miles away in South Australia and as it was Monday, they were already enrolled in a new school. For the third time in my life, I was struck by a shockwave of pain so intense that the ground slipped away and I felt all the lights go out.

This time at least, no-one had died, but nothing had prepared me for the shock of losing the boys to their father. I was not emotionally or mentally equipped to deal with the suddenness of the separation. It was like experiencing the loss of Crystal all over again – the empty beds, the abandoned toys and the instant yawning vacancy in my heart. Only this time, it was all my fault. Mick left me a note to explain his reasons. I felt so ashamed. He was right - I was not the person I used to be. I had turned into someone I hated. I could barely look at myself in the mirror. Still, I felt it wasn't right that he could just take my children without warning – especially after all that had happened in the past. But then again, I knew what I was doing with my life wasn't good either and Mick was right not to want the boys in harm's way. Once again, I hopped aboard my own personal rollercoaster of pain, guilt and grief. Once again, the black hole in my heart ripped wide open and threatened to engulf me. I wrote this poem to try to express the inexpressible:

Falling

That emptiness, that coldness
It's a deep black feeling
House it echos, sadness grows
Doesn't anybody want me?
Rejected, unloved , unnecessary
Doesn't anybody need me?
I tried, I failed, you took my heart
You took my life when you ripped my world apart
Aching inside, I am hollow and empty
How I love them, I love them how could you do this to me?

The silence is deafening , won't someone yell?
This is not my home I must be in hell
I stare at the floor, I stare at the ceiling
My world is rocking my head is reeling
Listening, listening, I can't hear their voice
Gone in the middle of the night left with no choice
I have nothing, you took everything
Oh how your words do cut, but your actions sting
Spinning and spinning, where has the light gone?
It was shiny, shiny but now the light's gone
Lord I'm sorry so sorry, may I have my light back?
Cause I am falling, falling into deep black
Help, help me turn back time please
Cause I am falling, falling
Yes I'm falling, falling!

I was in a lethal relationship with Nigel, drinking more than ever and now using drugs to get through the day. My car was dead with no way to pay the mechanic and I was weeks behind with the rent. With no job and any social security entitlement as a single mother wiped out in one fell swoop, I quickly became homeless. An acquaintance located a room for me close to the railway station. This living arrangement didn't last long as the man I was renting the room from had psychiatric problems and I was terrified of him. If I thought I had hit rock bottom before, now I was really there. I had no kids, no man, no home, no job, no money, no car, no friends, serious drug and alcohol problems and nobody to turn to.

Once again, a kind man entered my life and helped me to get back on my feet. Rebmen was unlike any other man I had ever been out with. His brown eyes were the friendliest I had seen in a long time and they were the only bright spot in a very dismal town. He was quiet and introverted and preferred his own company to anyone else's. We moved to a place called Plainlands where we had no social life and no friends, but that suited me fine. I couldn't face people anyway. My inbuilt rollercoaster had even broken down at this point and I just sunk lower and lower into one of the deepest depressions of my life. I blamed myself for the loss of not just one child but three. I felt so isolated and empty, a complete failure as a human being. I honestly began to feel that death was the only answer.

To top it all off, I began to hear voices.

Chapter 6

Backyard Blitz

"Mummy, mummy, your life is in danger!"

Thirteen years after her death, my daughter was calling
out to me. Aware of a chill swirling around me, I told
myself it was impossible - Crystal was long gone from this
world. But the voice was hers – clear and strong. To hear
it again after all these years was a shock to the system and
I'd had a gutful of shocks. It had been a terrible year. My
father was gone and my boys were half a continent away.
Mick had taken them to South Australia in August and it
was now November. We had been to Court on October
2nd, but because of school, the boys were to stay with
Mick until the next custody hearing in January. It had all
been such a mess and I wasn't sure I had enough left inside
me to make it through to January. I was deeply depressed
and thoughts of suicide invaded my mind on a daily basis.
"I've finally cracked," I thought to myself as I continued
to hear voices – first Crystal's and now a man's - speaking
to me as if they were right beside me.

"Charmaine, you aren't going crazy - this is real!" the
male voice assured me the first time I heard it.

"Who are you?" I asked, my ears pricking up to try to
identify exactly where the voice was coming from.

"I'm Peter." He had to be close, because he was
speaking in a whisper.

"Why are you whispering?" I asked, looking around the garden in an effort to pinpoint his hiding place. In disbelief, I saw what appeared to be ghosts swirling around in the yard. They were everywhere! I dashed inside, yelling for Rebmen to come and see.

"Come back inside and go to bed," Rebmen rolled his eyes at me, shaking his head, "there's nothing out there."

I thought Rebmen was probably right, perhaps I just needed glasses. But I kept looking anyway, very aware of this 'Peter' entity close by. He was still talking, but I couldn't make out the words. The more I tried to tune my ears to make sense out of the mumbling, the less I could understand. I couldn't catch any clear words at all and it was very frustrating.

"Speak up! I can't hear you." I hissed. I was trying to work out exactly where this stranger might be hiding - perhaps in the branches of a tree? I wondered what he was doing here, and how he knew my name. I was determined to find out. The mumbling continued as I wandered around the yard, mystified.

All of a sudden, the mumbling cleared and I heard Peter say, "Go to bed now."

With nothing better to do, I obeyed.

The following evening, I heard someone calling me to come outside. It was Peter. I sat on the step, and this time his voice was clearer as he asked me a few questions. The next thing I knew, the story of my life so far came pouring out, down the back steps and into the garden like a tidal wave. Peter listened to every word. I talked for ages, crying the whole time. I told him how much of a failure I felt and he listened, saying nothing. I talked his ears off and then, feeling a bit guilty for earbashing him, I asked him to tell me something about himself. Strangely, I 'felt' his answer rather than heard it. He said simply that he was happy to let me talk. So talk I did, well into the night. It was such a relief to have someone to confide in.

* * *

Over time, I noticed other voices and felt them coming from different areas. Some were kind like Pete, but others were obviously hostile and quite angry with me. I saw wispy figures everywhere, staying up for long hours just observing and trying to catch what they were saying. At times, I was convinced I could see them in the trees - if I looked closely enough, I could sometimes make out small figures in amongst the branches. These entities seemed to be able to levitate light objects, which made me suspect that somehow the whole thing was an elaborate set-up and the joke was on Charmaine, as usual. My imagination ran wild as I tried to figure out what magician's tricks might be at work. Perhaps halogen lights somehow projected these strange figures onto the backyard's landscape? I used mirrors and torches, shone spotlights into the trees to try to catch the tricksters out. When I got my hands on them, I'd show the culprits just what happens when you play with somebody's mind in such a cruel way. But of course, I never uncovered their hiding place.

Quite often, I would sense the entities' presence by sighting lights. Blue balls of light would gravitate smoothly through the air towards me. In my ignorance, I didn't realise this was spiritual activity. I kept trying to figure out where the lights were coming from - were they connected to the trees? Something up above? What the hell were these blue balls that never got close enough for me to touch? They stayed against the fence-line and would move as I moved. I could see the blue balls of light during the day and at night. I tried to get photographs of them, but I could never capture one on film. (I do, however, have a lovely collection of tree photos to remind me of that time!)

Nobody else could see anything so I gave up asking people to look. I worried for my sanity, I really did, and I wasn't the only one. I worried that all the years of abusing my body were catching up with me and I was having hallucinations or some kind of psychotic episode, but somehow I knew on a deep level that there was much more to it than that. I'd been around long enough to know this was something different. I was fascinated. I lost a lot of sleep but I didn't care - I had to work out some sort of explanation for the mysterious things I was seeing. Were they real people, projections, or what? I must say that it was driving me crazy. I needed a way to process and understand what was happening, but as ever, there were no immediate answers.

These entities were with me constantly. I could feel them watching me and sense them wherever I went. I was very confused. I would look in the mirror and see different faces, or my own face would look like it was dissolving. There was a constant ringing in my ears. The closer the entities were, the louder the ringing noise became. My mouth was constantly dry whenever they were near. It was a total mystery. Yes, I felt nuts but I was seeing, hearing and feeling all of these things while going about my daily business. Somehow, I knew I was not mad, I just knew it. A voice kept assuring me, "This is real!" I'm not sure if that voice was Pete's or my own, but I believed it. All the evidence was there, I just couldn't comprehend what was happening to me in any logical way.

As the spirit world opened up before my eyes, I would actually see figures before me on the grass. On windless nights, these entities would shake the clothesline violently. I could see the clothes shaking and swishing, when not a breath of wind moved the leaves in the trees. It was like something or someone was putting on a performance designed to wake me up to another reality. My brain struggled to make sense of it − I was still partly convinced that the neighbours or maybe some local kids were having a laugh at my expense, using holograms or projectors and fishing line to create optical illusions. But if that was the case, then other people would have seen what I was seeing. I spent many hours in the backyard trying to figure it out, but try as I might, I could never find any props or evidence to explain my experiences.

At that time, I only ever heard things outside, never in the house. Although I had seen things in the mirror or on the walls, there was no sound. It seemed like the voices would only ever speak to me when I was in the backyard. I feel now that it was part of their plan to make me wake up to myself, get outside in the fresh air and straighten out my ways.

* * *

It's very important that I pause here to talk a bit about the role of drugs and alcohol in this whole experience. I have often been asked (and certainly did wonder at the time) if what I was experiencing could simply be attributed to some kind of drug-related psychosis. Certainly, many of the experiences I had in those days fit neatly into the category of chemical side-effects. Perhaps some of the things I experienced were just the drugs or the alcohol talking, but at the time I instinctively knew there was more to it. Still, how would I ever know for sure if I didn't stop interfering with my own sanity by writing myself off? In my case, the confusion and fear that surrounded my early experiences with spirit disappeared when I stopped abusing my body. But instead of the entities disappearing, they demanded more from me. They demanded I stay focussed and present in the 'now', taking care of my health so that I could become an effective and clear channel. Cleansed and healthy, taking responsibility for myself at last, I can now easily distinguish which experiences were the work of spirit and which were the effects of the chemicals in my system at that time.

But only in retrospect.

I was very lucky. I now understand that spirit intervened to stop me from self-destructing, using all the circus tricks in the book to distract me from my addiction problems. Substance abuse played a role in my spiritual awakening, but only in the sense that spirit stepped in to save me from myself at the lowest ebb of my life. I should add here that spirit did not float down from the sky and gently lift me up on silver wings to a better way of living. Spirit kicked my arse! Spirit called me every name in the book. Spirit promised to meet me at the gates of death and kick my arse even harder for all eternity if I didn't clean up my act and start living. Spirit slagged me off, taunted me, laughed at me and confirmed all the bad things I thought about myself every minute of the day until I woke up.

"Mummy, mummy – your life is in danger!"
Spirit, in the form of my beautiful daughter Crystal, begged me to take notice. I woke up. And spirit, in the form of my closest guide, Pete, was there to help me find my way out of the mess and towards a meaningful life. But it didn't happen overnight, and it wasn't pretty.

I cannot stress strongly enough, knowing what I know now, that abusing drugs of any kind only gets in the way of spiritual work. If you are taking drugs and experiencing hallucinations of any kind, this does not mean you are becoming a medium. If you are contemplating using drugs to 'open the doors of perception', think again! You may well have a profound spiritual experience while in an artificially altered state of reality, but how can you understand its meaning if you are off your face? In my experience, confusion and fear were heightened and authentic communication with spirit was diminished whenever I drank or took drugs. Spirit was talking to me and I was hunting for kids with a torch! It was only when I stopped using all addictive substances and approached the issue with the respect it deserved, that clear positive communication with spirit became possible. From my current perspective, I'd recommend anyone seeking to communicate with spirit leave 'spirits' of the alcoholic variety as well as any other mind-altering substances out of the equation!

* * *

Mick and I went to court in January and the judge ordered that the boys be brought back to South East Queensland. I was able to have them with me again, but only every second weekend and for half the school holidays. I was ecstatic that my boys would be close by, but the victory was only a partial one as I had hoped they would be returned to me full-time. Instead, it seemed they were happy with their Dad. It was a blow. By the time I arrived home from the hearing, my elation had been replaced by a dark depression. Rebmen was never a great comforter, finding it difficult to know what to say or do for me at times like these. When we arrived home, he was content to let me sit out back and process the day's events alone. I settled on the back steps and Peter talked me through it. Rebmen made it very clear that he thought I was hearing things because I was mad.

No one was happy with me at all. My whole family thought I had flipped, except for my youngest son, Jack. Thank God for Jack! He was the only one who backed me and loved me unconditionally in those dark days. He was also the only one who confirmed the sightings I had. I can't describe the relief I felt when I would point out the 'people' and he told me he could see them too! More than just agreeing with me because he loved me, Jack could accurately point out where they were. Thanks to Jack, I kept my sanity. He was my saviour in all the madness. His innocent belief and trust in me then is the chief reason I'm still alive today. That's not an exaggeration, I was still so deeply depressed that I just couldn't see a light at the end of the tunnel. Sure, plenty of blue balls of light flying around in the yard, but that was more of a burden at that time than a blessing. Lying on the couch and searching the trees by day, then scanning the skies and listening for the voices at night was not doing me any good. I couldn't take it any more. I began to express out loud my wish to get my life back together...

"Do you want me to give you a job?" said Peter who was listening as usual.

"Yes!" God did I ever.

"You'll have to make a lot of changes if you want to work for me," he warned.

"I can do whatever you need me to do," I assured him. I needed a job to get my mind off things. Even though I had the kids regularly, I was still very unsettled and unhappy with my past choices and could not pull myself together. From past experience, good old fashioned hard work was the best medicine, and it came in the form of 'chicken poop for the soul' once again. In March 2000, I got a job working at a chicken farm.

The job was dirty, smelly and horrifying at first. Talk about coming back down to earth. It poured with rain on my first day, and when I entered the chook shed I was bowled over by the smell. Picture for a moment a large shed containing six thousand chickens and fifteen hundred roosters, all roaming free. My task was to walk around the shed amongst the chooks and pick up floor eggs. This might sound fairly easy, but as well as bending over at least 1000 times to pick the eggs up off the floor, I had to come quickly to terms with the fact that roosters attack you if you show fear. Believe me, I felt fear that first day! Every five seconds, a vicious rooster leapt at me, pecking ferociously at my legs. My nerves were already shot to pieces, so I was overwhelmed by the job at first. Eventually I got used to it and was promoted to egg picker and given my own shed, where I trained the chickens to lay eggs on the nest and not on the floor. I loved my chooks and they loved me back. I gave quite a few of them names. Chickens are nice creatures and although I wouldn't like to do that job again, I'm glad that I did. It was time out from a bad period in my life. A time spent getting back to the earth.

The chicken job was hard work. I stopped going out the back at night. I was simply too tired to be bothered taking photos of what I knew would turn out to be just more trees. I didn't feel the need to go out to talk to Peter most of the time - usually I just could not keep my eyes open beyond 7.30 pm. I was up again at 5 am and at work by 6.30 in the morning. Strangely enough, the times I did try to find Peter, he wasn't there. I thought about him a lot though. I missed him. I wanted to thank him for getting me off my bum and back into a more human routine. I put Peter out of my mind and concentrated on salvaging my relationship with the boys while building one with 6000 chooks. Then I slipped on another emotional banana-skin.

On the 27th of June 2000, I went to see the court counsellor about the possibility of getting the boys back full-time. He told me in no uncertain terms that I would never get them back unless the boys themselves made the decision to live with me. They were happy with their father and had expressed that my constant crying and begging them to return home was, shall we say, unappealing. They just wanted their old mum back.

June 28th 2000. Crystal had been dead for fourteen years and the realisation had finally dawned that my boys would probably never come home to live with me. I had given birth to three wonderful children and none of them were by my side. In time-honoured fashion, I wiped myself out to numb the pain. I kept my job another two days or so until the holidays started. Although I had worked hard and enjoyed the chicken job, when the company refused to give me time off to be with my kids over the school holidays, I simply left. It was too important for me. After the holidays, when the kids went home, all the old feelings of failure swamped over me at full force. I handled it the way I always had – by intoxicating myself to the max. Before long, I was a complete mess again and thoughts of suicide returned. This went on for about a week before Peter was back on the scene.

Disappointed and angry that I was back to my old tricks trying to drown my sorrows, Peter once again talked me through it. He had help from a lot of different voices, and what some of them said absolutely terrified me. I knew I had to break the patterns of a lifetime but I just couldn't seem to find the inner strength to do it. A battle was going on for my sanity and my life, and I knew it. I was hysterical most of the time. I tried to get another job and actually succeeded, but left after only one night of work. I was tired, scared and just deeply sad. Rebmen was completely fed up with me and worried about my constant 'talking to myself'. He seriously began to consider having me committed for psychiatric treatment. When he started talking about straightjackets and padded rooms, I knew it was time to make one last huge effort to get back on track and straighten out. As usual, once the decision was made, Peter supported me all the way. This time, it had only taken six weeks before I pulled myself up again. For me, that was a huge improvement.

Chapter 7

Wake Up!

Despite all my efforts to do the right thing and straighten myself up, the underlying depression just wouldn't lift. While I'd been working at the chook factory, I'd kept away from drugs entirely and cut right back on the drinking during the week. After I left the job and the kids went home, I didn't immediately return to the old patterns, it was more that I found I just couldn't get motivated. Mostly I just slept, watched television and sat around feeling sorry for myself until the boys were due to visit. This went on for months. Every two weeks, I would shake myself off the couch and put a smile on my face so the boys wouldn't realise how sad I was. They wanted their old mum back and although I didn't know where she was, I tried hard to imitate her. Slowly, they began to feel comfortable and trust me again. I felt I didn't deserve it, but kids being kids, they still loved me. It had been a slow, long and hard road but I was succeeding. I still went on pain-blocker drinking binges occasionally, but tried hard to keep the truth hidden from the kids.

Inch by inch, I began to feel better and I got a job in April of 2001 which I kept until I moved house in August that same year. In July, the voices and visions came back with a force. This time it was not just Peter, there were more. He was there, but there were others. They were so loud that it was affecting my sleep. I would just drop off and they would yell to wake me up. I was getting scared now. There was nothing I could do to stop them. I began getting intoxicated more frequently to try to drown them out. The more I drank, the worse they yelled. I could not make them go away. We even moved house in an attempt to get away from them (Rebmen was still prepared to humour me to get a bit of peace) but the entities just followed. They were worse than ever. 'Wake up!" they would yell, over and over again. I would scream back that I was awake and punch wildly at the air.

I looked at the wall and saw faces. I looked at the carpet and saw faces. I would look out the back and see figures that would always disappear when anyone else came near. Some of the entities became abusive, calling me horrible names. So I drank more and more hoping to rid myself of their presence. I was in a nightmare that was hard for anyone to understand. Imagine being able to hear up to seven people telling you that you were never going to amount to anything. The abuse was 24/7. Believe me, there was not much sleep. I searched frantically for Peter's kind voice but it seemed he was nowhere to be found. When everything got really bad, he would come and put an end to the nasty voices and then finally sleep would overtake my exhausted mind. They usually eased up when the kids came over, a bit anyway. I had to pretend nothing was wrong when I was in company and it was so hard.

Up until that time, I had only ever heard voices outside the house but now I heard them everywhere - in the house, in the supermarket, at McDonalds - you name it. I was terrified most of the time. The voices now talked to me through television shows. They distracted me constantly. I could even hear them through the speakers in my car stereo. The strange light activity increased too. I remember sitting in the lounge room in the dark one night and seeing all these blue beams of light criss-crossing the room. I thought that if I crawled under the beams, *Mission Impossible*-style, they wouldn't be able to 'get' me. (How the spirits must have laughed at me crawling across the floor!) It was no laughing matter to me though. I was convinced that if the blue lights shone on me, I was done for.

I cracked under the pressure and returned to drugs to try to wipe myself out. Of course, this didn't help matters one bit. The abuse became intolerable – some of the entities jeered at me and told me I should just go ahead and kill myself, because I was living a worthless life anyway. I really thought I was going to die and in the end, I was hospitalised because my blood pressure was ridiculously high - 280/180. It was my mother's birthday and it was a really terrible time because I knew I had lost all grasp of reality at this stage. None of my old pain-blocking tricks were working anymore – alcohol and drugs didn't give me relief from the constant harassment or even an artificial security blanket. All my attempts to escape from reality just made things ten times worse. My own thoughts mingled with the constant chatter in my head and everything was even more jumbled and distorted when I was out of it. I knew I had reached a dead end. There was nothing paranormal about being rushed to hospital - that was down to my habits. I couldn't always be sure at that point what was real and what wasn't. Now I know without a doubt that during all the mess and confusion of that time, the spirits never left me. At the scariest moments, a little voice would sing the words of Bob Marley, "Every little thing's...gonna be alright." That little voice was Crystal's.

The abuse from the other voices was vicious and constant, but that sweet little voice just kept on singing. I hung on to it for dear life through the days that followed.

September 11th, 2001

I began the day in a daze. I hadn't liked myself for a very long time and was off my face as usual. I remember turning on the television and every channel was showing the same news footage over and over: planes smashing into gleaming buildings; the giant Twin Towers falling and disintegrating into dust; images of fear, death and tears. I watched it all through a haze, unable to compute the reality of what I was seeing. I remember trying to change the channel, but all were the same – replaying the events over and over again. It was surreal, like some sick 'Groundhog Day'. I just couldn't escape the images of impact and destruction. Through the daze, I recognised what was happening as a metaphor for my life. Change the channel and watch everything fall to bits all over again. No matter how many times I had changed the channel in my life, the footage was the same. And here I was, standing in the wreckage yet again.

"Wake Up!" the voices yelled at me. I turned the television off.

On television the following day, I saw a group of beautiful young Iraqis sitting on a lawn somewhere. All of them had lit candles for the victims of the terrorist attacks in New York. I realised then that some of those young Iraqis were likely to pay a huge personal price for the terrorist attacks in the days that followed. There was nothing psychic about that, I guess like many people, I understood that the Americans in their grief and outrage would need to take revenge and bomb someone. The odds were that Iraq would suffer for what Al Qaeda had done, whether they had anything to do with it or not.

I suddenly realised that 9/11, all the wars before and to come were just part of the same destructive cycle - the cycle of grief. I understood, really understood for the first time, that actions like terrorist attacks and the various wars we see unfolding every day are built on grief. The need to relieve the pain usually ends up creating more grief for everyone. The impact of that realisation was very powerful. It began to dawn on me that my own self-destructive patterns were part of this same cycle of grief. I had a strong sense that I was waking up, realising that the world had all changed, and things weren't the same as they'd been when I 'went to sleep' so many years ago. I had compassion for the people who had been killed on 9/11 but strangely, I felt in my heart that those people were ok. It was the rest of the world that wasn't – and like it or not, I was a part of that world.

Out of habit, I poured myself a large drink to help me digest this sudden insight. Lifting the glass to my lips, I became aware of Peter's presence in the room. I could feel him watching me intensely.

"What are you looking at?" I demanded.

"I'm watching you abuse yourself for the last time," he said matter-of-factly.

I knew he was right. I took my last drink on September the 12th and stopped using drugs once and for all. I decided that day that I was going to change forever.

I finally woke up.

* * *

I went to stay with my sister in Toowoomba to sort myself out. The voices followed me there. Although they had become kinder now that I was making the effort to get myself sorted out once and for all, they still wouldn't let me sleep. One female voice and several males talked to me about my life, my beliefs, my alcohol, my friends, my mother, my father and myself as a mother. I think I'd have been lucky to get three or four hours' sleep a night. Despite the fact that I was completely straight, I would still see them everywhere: at the gym, at Picnic Point in the trees and all over the place.

Rebmen and I split up not long afterwards. I needed space to clear my life of all the baggage I had attached to myself over the years. When he left, I started to get my act together. I joined an aerobics class again and was very well-behaved. I was trying to give up the ciggies and was eating well for the first time in years. Peter had become a fixture in my life, helping me to make the long-overdue changes. The other voices were still around, but now they were not so horrid. They still talked non-stop and kept me awake at night but it was not as hard as it had been. It seemed that everywhere I went, they were with me. I could hear the different tones of their voices and it was hard to hold a conversation of my own at times, as they would happily insert their own views on any topic at the most inappropriate times! I had imagined that once I started getting healthy, all the paranormal events would just disappear. Many of the 'horror sequences' became a thing of the past, it's true. But I understand now that the voices, especially those of Peter and Crystal, had stepped in to help me get back on track. They were not symptoms of my self-destructive habits, but the solution to them. When I began to listen to them and not just 'hear' them, things began to improve quite rapidly.

By October, money was very tight. Peter told me I would get a job the next day, if I called the Air Force base canteen and asked for a man named Steve. I had nothing to lose, so I gave it a shot and to my surprise, I did get a job immediately, driving the smoko van around the base! Well, Peter's detailed knowledge of the personnel situation at the base had me convinced that he was somehow connected to the military. How else would he know about the van-driving job? It was the only thing that made sense! Peter told me that I would work for a while and then, after he had 'trained me', I would work with him. I would be his 'partner in life'. Partner in life? "What the hell is that supposed to mean?", I thought to myself. I came to the conclusion that somehow this man, Peter, was accessing my mind through ESP and once my 'powers' were developed, I would be put to work in a secret psychic branch of the military. At first, I thought that these guys had succeeded in scaring me straight, and therefore they wanted my assistance to scare other people. I thought I was part of some elaborate experiment. It did seem far-fetched even to me, but it was the only explanation that made any sense at the time. I found a book on psychic phenomena at a Target book sale not long after I got the job at the base. Inside was a whole section devoted to psychic warfare. A short paragraph about remote viewing and mind control in the US military confirmed all my suspicions. I began to prepare for the inevitable meeting with my mystery recruiter, Peter.

The Healers

Locked in boxes with dark locks , It was your feelings
Deep dark secrets, interfering with your healings,
We would not tell, of your lonely hell
World you know too well
Cos we're not talking, we are listening
You walked through one door, you slammed another,
*   how it echoed*
You left it open, It was a window and they followed
Nightmares and memories too
Look how they coloured you
We can see right through
But we're not talking, we are listening
Hear us whisper, you're not crazy, do you understand
There are no answers, do you fear us, are you trusting?
Cos we will drag you through.
Every hell that belongs to you
and you will pay your dues
But we're not talking, we are listening
Boxes unlocked, world is waiting , we have called you
If you stand tall there is one thing we will tell you
You have one choice, to hear our voice
and it would be wise, if you stopped talking
Are you listening to me?

Chapter 8

Psychic Boot Camp

My 'training' began in earnest after that. The more telepathic I thought I was, the more I tried to improve my ability, communicating with six or seven voices at a time.

Still thinking that I was part of a military experiment, I listened to my 'trainers' with an image in my mind of men in uniform sitting around a table, talking to me through some kind of secret communication device. They would get me to look at someone in the supermarket and try to tune into them to what they were thinking. The more I practised, the better I became. I started to 'read' people all the time - at the supermarket, at work, in fact everywhere I went. I remember one day at the checkout, I could just tell this young fellow wanted to be working on his car rather than in a supermarket queue. Somehow I also knew he had blockages in the fuel system of his car. So, as you do, I just blurted all this information out to him. He told me I was right – he was preoccupied by problems with his car and was in a hurry to get back to it so he could figure out why it wasn't running properly. He couldn't understand how I knew about the fuel blockages, but that was what he was planning to check next. I was mystified myself. I could hear the voices mumbling in the background through this whole conversation. (I don't tune into people at random anymore - I feel it is quite invasive - but it was all part of the learning process.)

As I actively developed my 'tuning in' skills, other aspects of psychic ability caught me by surprise. I didn't understand everything that was happening, but I recognised things as they occurred. I would drive to work and somehow by the time I got there, I would know everything that would be said to me when I arrived. Another day as I was driving to work, Peter or one of the others just said out of the blue, "Remember that little ginger kitten you and Crystal weaned?" What? I couldn't remember ever talking about that to anyone. I had forgotten it myself, it was so many years ago. How could the military know about those sorts of details? I got all teary eyed. Besides me, only Crystal would have remembered that kitten.

Around this time, as part of the healing process, I started to write music and play guitar again. I had put the guitar down when Crystal died and then again when the boys left. The songs practically wrote themselves once I picked up the guitar again. The words were flowing and it felt so good to get them out. I could literally feel the healing effect of my own music as the days passed. Each sentence had so much meaning that the pain inside gradually began to lessen once the feelings were expressed. I wrote about my kids, my addiction, how the boys' father made me feel, about war and society. I put music to all these songs. There were songs of inspiration too. In a three-month period, I wrote ten songs. It was like I had opened a floodgate - I just couldn't stop. In hindsight, I realise the importance of that time and how deeply healing the music was. I also understand now that some of the songs were words from spirit and I treasure them all. Peter enjoyed my music and was never far from my side.

All the while, the psychic 'training program' continued. By January 2002, the training sessions had become very intense. Peter was teaching me to block my thoughts and to follow the flow of his words. It was like drawing patterns in my head. The patterns were trains of words. He told me to think in my pinkie toe because he did not want to hear my thoughts. If I did think when he was speaking to me, my thought would echo over and over in my head like a squash ball bouncing off a wall. It was horrible!

"DON'T THINK!" Peter would command me. I tried so hard not to think, I was angry with him for inflicting these mental exercises on me. It was really torture to discipline my mind! I hadn't asked for any of this and I was really doing the best I could. I mean, not only did I have to hear all their stuff but now, my own thoughts were being pushed away. It was like being a hostage in my own mind. Like in meditation, the more you try to tune out your thoughts, the more you think about not thinking and it can be quite frustrating. It was really hard to do and let's face it, I wasn't the most mentally disciplined.

Peter would tell me to 'block his words'. I would think 'BLOCK' and then I would hear 'Block, Block, Block' echo over and over in my head. It was a nightmare. I really began to resent this man. My trainers would push me as far as my temper or patience could take it, then they'd pull back and throw me a comfort pillow. Just when I thought I couldn't take it another second, a familiar little voice would start singing, '*Every little thing's gonna be alright*'. But they had to keep pushing me and they did. Through all this time, I was healing, healing, healing. I kept writing those extraordinary songs often in one hit, and despite the frustrations, I gave my full attention to the lessons I was receiving.

I faced up to a lot of things at that time. A very important aspect of the healing process was to acknowledge the part *I* had played in the path my life had taken. I had to look in 'the mirror' and realise I was responsible for the things that had happened to me and for my reaction to them. In April 2002, I invited Crystal's father over to make peace with him. It took a lot of organising but we made the effort - our first contact face to face in 16 years - and by the time he left, we had given a lot of old wounds permission to heal. It did me a lot of good, and I hope it benefited him in the same way. To forgive him in my heart, to openly hug him and say, "let's put all this crap behind us" was very liberating. Not just on the surface but deep in my heart, I had to forgive all the people I felt had hurt me, including Mick for taking the kids. I had to come to the understanding that had I been in his shoes, I would have done the same thing. I couldn't say 'poor me, stupid me' – I had played an active role in everything that had happened. My life didn't just happen to me. To accept my responsibility was enlightening.

No Doubt

I remember you from long ago
We did time in the old school
I was so very much younger then
And, O boy, did I make you drool
I had magic in my brown eyes
And a smile I kept just for you
But as the years slipped by
The world it rocked us
I know where I went
What happened to you

Charmaine Wilson

You seem so cold and hard
Did I break your heart
If I did, I didn't mean to
But I didn't want to be
That bitter, angry woman I became
I wanted to stay the young girl
That would seduce you
So I wasn't hanging around
To cop your mental and physical abuse
And oh by the way
Whatever happened to that sexy young man
That used to make me feel so
Naughty and beautiful
All at the same time

Well we just froze each other's hearts
Forgot how to laugh
And our world, it split in two
Then we took each other's worlds
Kicked them to the sky and watched our lives fall out.

Here we stand in the stomping grounds
Of our youth, will time ever heal
And I wonder as I look into your eyes
Which of us really got the better deal
As I offer my hand of friendship, you hesitate
And my blood, it runs a little cold
Cos we're united by a young lovers' pact
By our kin, until we grow old.

I was attracting all kinds of men at that time, but my guides weren't having it. I had to leave my 'inner alley cat' behind and focus. I felt very exposed, being aware that the entities could see my behaviours. With someone watching me, I had to take a fresh look at the notion of right and wrong. I was turned off sex for two years because of the intensity of facing myself and the intrusiveness of the spirits. I'm used to it now but it took time. In fact, I am grateful for the awareness of spirit around me these days. I'm still plagued by cravings for cigarettes and alcohol, but the sense of responsibility I feel towards people who are grieving and those who look to me for inspiration helps me to make the right choices. Quite honestly, on the odd occasion that I have slipped and had a few sneaky puffs of a cigarette or a glass of beer, my guides made their disapproval pretty clear.

Peter spent a lot of time teaching me to clear my mind. He was also teaching me to 'listen' with my whole body. It was working too. If I went to work and someone had a pain somewhere, I could always locate it. I was still seeing things on the walls and floors if I stared long enough. They looked like faces changing; the main face being a fellow with a beard and glasses. I thought this may have been Peter but couldn't figure out how he got the face to appear wherever I looked. I would ask him where he was and his reply was always the same: "Right in front of you!"

I thought he was being a 'smart-arse'. I wanted to know where his office was at the base. At night when I closed my eyes, strange visions would appear that looked like pictures on water at first. In them was always this man with a *Fu Manchu* moustache. He would be driving a car or just walking around. It was all very strange. Was Peter the guy with the moustache?

I kept asking if we could meet and he always said, "not yet". I was really confused. You see, I had been through such hell that I was missing the obvious. If I'd understood then that Peter was a spirit, I could have saved myself a lot of time and confusion. Instead, I would walk down the street and look at normal people and envy them. I started to wonder what it would be like with no noise in your head, nobody talking all the time. I would cry at work some days and have to run to the bathroom to hide my tears. I had nobody to confide in. I thought I was in training for psychic warfare for the army and was afraid to blow it. I just couldn't understand why I had to wait so long for a formal interview. I had been just a normal but sad woman before all these voices started. I was totally out of my depth. I needed to find a reasonable explanation for everything that was happening and because of the job I had driving the smoko van at the air force base, the military explanation was the only reasonable one for my mind to cling to. It was hard to live in a world where you never quite knew what was real.

I was still seeing 'people' in the distance I thought were guys in combat gear. At night in the backyard, I would look up and hear noises: 'beep beep beep'. Because at this stage I was so deeply convinced the army were trying to recruit me for a psychic spy job, I thought the beeping was the sound of someone pedalling a gyrocopter over the trees! I would hear the beeping and think, "there he goes". I had it all worked out - these dudes were up in their gyrocopters, or in a hot air balloon flying over the trees, which would explain why I heard those twigs breaking - no it wouldn't be the possums at all! It was such a crazy time in my life. When I think back now, I can see when the entities tried to explain that they were spirits but while I was living it, I just could not comprehend. In my heart now, I feel all the pain and grief I had gone through left me with a deep need to believe that I had something of value to offer the world. I needed to feel that someone wanted me, that there was a purpose to all the things I had experienced. If I had what it took to be the ideal military guinea-pig, then at least that meant I was going to be useful to somebody.

By February 2002, money had become very tight. I was anxious all of the time. My rent was behind by about a month. Luckily, I had an understanding landlord who allowed me to do some work for him to pay off the debt. He spray-painted cars and boats so I helped him by sanding them down. I still had a lot of debts hanging over my head, worrying constantly about where the money was going to come from. Once again, Peter came through – he was a terrific employment consultant! Peter told me to go to Ipswich and walk up the main street. He said I would find a shop with a sign in the window advertising for a tarot card reader. If I applied, he told me, I would get the job. Well, he was right as usual and I started working the following Thursday. I still had the tarot cards I had bought through the book club just after Crystal died, so I dug them out of the cupboard and dusted them off.

Although I had used them before when I was searching for Crystal, as I started working with the tarot cards again, there was definitely more clarity and a higher degree of accuracy than before. I felt a bit like someone cheating at poker though, because I now had a bit of help. The voices told me things about the client sitting in front of me, which always turned out to be true. I gave psychometry readings too, with similar results. One day, I was out the front of the shop talking to the owner when she suggested I hold her ring to see what came up. The reading I gave her astounded us both. A bit later a woman came in and I held her ring which revealed to me that she was having an affair with two married men. That totally blew her mind – and mine too, if I'm honest!

Once during a reading for a female client, I repeatedly heard the name 'Rose'. I also had a very vivid impression of the Snowy Mountains - essentially I 'felt' them. The client told me that she had an Aunt Rose with whom she went to the Snowy Mountains, but had died some time ago. I was a little confused. At this stage, I knew practically nothing about mediums or contacting the spirit world – to be honest that side of the psychic world just didn't really register on my radar. I had used the ouija board all those years before, but I never really understood or had much faith in the process. As kids, it was more of a daring parlour game and we always assumed someone in the room was moving the cup.

So, connecting the voices in my head with the spirits of people who had passed away just never occurred to me at the time. I was still trying to figure out what lay ahead of me in the world of psychic espionage and military mind control. I thought everything I was doing was some kind of scientific experiment and that Peter and the others would show up in uniform someday soon to reveal it all. I needed to believe there was a more mundane or scientific explanation for what was happening to me, because at the time I was unaware of any alternative other than mental illness. I refused to entertain the idea that I was mentally ill – I'd battled too hard for my sanity. I'd lost pretty much everything I'd ever cared about, but I was determined not to lose my mind without a hell of a fight. Still, I was very worried about the voices I was hearing as they seemed to come from outside of me at times and from inside of me at other times. The covert military explanation was the most plausible one but surely by now someone would have physically approached me. I knew I was being 'tested' in some way, but what use would I be to anyone if they drove me nuts in the process of training me? I needed to confide in someone, so in desperation I sought advice from one of the other clairvoyants who worked at the shop.

The clairvoyant sat calmly back in his chair, closed his eyes and smiled as he listened to my story. I asked him if he thought it was possible that the voices I was hearing were from the military. The clairvoyant calmly reassured me that I wasn't insane. He gently explained that no, it wasn't a covert military recruitment exercise I had been experiencing, there was a much simpler and more profound explanation. Lowering his voice to a whisper, he informed me that I was communicating with a *fourteen-foot space alien*. Now, you might well imagine that I laughed out loud at this explanation. Far from it! My mind frantically went through everything I had seen and heard. It all became so painfully clear. Suddenly all the unanswerable questions were answered! At last, I had found an explanation that covered all bases - space aliens! Of course! Why hadn't I picked it? It all made sense! This is why there were strange blue orbs of light, laser beams in the lounge room, visions of other worlds, voices from inside and outside. Alien technology made all this possible. Peter wasn't some mind-control expert in uniform speaking to me from the military base. He was a highly developed being communicating with me from outer space. It wasn't the military who were going to come for me when my training was complete – it was a spaceship!

I left the shop that day with a spring in my step. I had my answer. I couldn't thank the clairvoyant enough. Naturally, he warned me not to tell anyone about what he'd revealed as none would have believed me and it might jeopardise the great alien mission. I was sworn to secrecy or goodness knows what might happen…

So now instead of searching the trees, I began to search the skies night and day. My imagination was going crazy with the possibilities. This revelation occurred around the time of CHOGM. Living as close as I did to the airforce base, there was a lot of activity as the servicemen practiced night and day security tactics. So there I was, out on my back verandah looking at the skies and imagining that each and every one of the aircraft I saw was a spaceship about to land and take me away. At night, as I drove down the highway and my car headlights hit distant reflectors in the middle of the road, I was convinced they were hovering UFOs. Naturally, I would stop and look up, see nothing and get angry. Damned space aliens!

I used to lie awake in bed at night and talk with my fourteen-foot friend. (The spirits must have had a ball with me at this time!) The bedtime conversations went something like this:

"We're going to come down and we're going to take you…"

"What? Am I going to be dead??"

"No, Charmaine"

"But what about Jack?"

"Well, we're going to take Jack too someday"

"But you can't take *Jack*."

I didn't mind about me, but I wasn't keen about Jack being whisked off in a spaceship to another planet – he hadn't even finished school!

"When are you going to come for me?" I asked, scared to death.

"When the time comes, it will happen. And we're going to take that clairvoyant too."

Looking back, I think the spirits were a bit cranky that the male clairvoyant had told me they were space aliens. When I reflect on it, I think he must have known what was really happening – he was a very experienced practitioner who regularly did readings at a spiritualist church. Perhaps he was somehow threatened by my early abilities, and tried to put me off the track, I don't know. Much later, I visited the spiritualist church where he was reverend and offered to do readings for his psychic fair. On that day, spirits were coming through one after the other. I looked over at the clairvoyant afterwards and he was absolutely seething with anger. He didn't speak to me at all for the rest of the day. Clearly, he was dismayed that the messages I had relayed had brought tears to the eyes of their recipients. It was obvious he felt 'outdone'. I took a distance from spirituality after that - I had gone to him for help and he told me I was communicating with space aliens. He had never really wanted to help me, and if that's what being spiritual meant, he could shove it!

Now, where was I? Oh yes, space aliens. Through all this confusion, I had kept contact with Rebmen and when

I started going on about space aliens, well, he just laughed and laughed, told me I had finally and completely lost it and immediately tried to change the subject. I think he was seriously worried. I even told him I thought they were going to come and get me and take me to another planet. Now he'd heard it all. For my part, I was very scared on one hand and relieved on the other. You see, life to me was not a bed of roses and never had been. So as far as I was concerned, if it was better elsewhere, then *bring it on*. I was game.

In the meantime, here I was again, on the edge of insanity, looking for spaceships and totally depressed. I had certainly come a long way since 911, confronting myself, dealing with issues of forgiveness and so on. Healing was certainly happening in many ways. The problem was that I still couldn't come to grips with who these voices were that were behind it all. The advice about space aliens certainly did nothing to help me find clarity. Now, although I don't want to criticize anyone or scoff at his or her beliefs, I really do not believe that I was ever communicating with a 14-foot space alien. At the time, I believed it with all my heart but I can quite honestly say the information nearly destroyed my sanity once and for all. I am not saying that we are the only life form in the universe, but I am an advocate of believing what I can prove to myself. Until the day I see that 14-foot alien stand before me, I will never believe that I am communicating with one. I hope I haven't offended anyone with these comments but this is how I feel on the subject. I would urge anyone to check and re-check any information that does not sit right or causes undue stress. Believe me when I say it is worthwhile getting a second or third opinion.

Yin Yang

Crazy hazy mixed up days of youth
Paint the picture between tame and uncouth
Were you ridden on a rough road much too long
Are you crazy? Are you lazy ? Are you strong?

Did you ride a silver spoon to the moon
Or did society push you out way too soon
Did you lay down in a gold plated bed
Did tragedy turn your green light to red

Do you wallow in the blues
Think of everything you had to lose
Do you stand up for your right
Take the day while you ride the night
Do you respect yourself or
Are you detrimental to your health
Does passion take control
Or is it love that makes you whole?

The future is written in your past
Life is short, don't live too fast
It's your life only you can choose
Will you win or will you lose
It's a yin yang mentality
A fine line of insanity,
The dividing line of society
Two faced, double edged
Upside down, crazy land
What in the hell do you do demand
And are you going to receive
Do you Believe?

Chapter 9

The Penny Drops

Thoughts of aliens and psychic spies invaded my life for another two months before someone else came along and offered me another option. This person not only turned my life around but completely changed the way I thought about everything. I turned on the television one day, and there he was: a good-looking bloke with a mouth that spoke at a thousand miles an hour. This man was John Edward, the psychic medium, and he was working in front of a studio audience. He was speaking to one audience member after the other, giving them validation after validation that their loved ones were safe and happy on the other side. It seemed in fact that they were right there in the room next to them. There were tears and laughter from the people involved and the whole audience joined in. Right there on television, grief-stricken people changed before my eyes.

After John Edward left the stage, audience members he had spoken to were given the opportunity to tell the viewers how their loved ones had 'crossed over' and how this psychic medium had changed their lives forever. They didn't really need to say he had changed their lives - it was clearly written all over their faces. I stood in front of the television with my mouth hanging open until the credits rolled. I was amazed that the spirit world could be reached in such a way. Where had this guy been when my loved ones had crossed over? If only he had been around then, my life might have turned out very differently. I thought about the readings I had been doing. Wasn't the process John Edward used essentially what I had been experiencing? From what I could see, he was receiving information from sources in the spirit world and passing it directly on to the intended receiver....

Peter and the other voices - military men/space aliens - had watched the show with me and it now seemed they were very excited.... The chattering and babbling became almost deafening.....

....and the penny finally dropped.

My 'trainers' were *spirits* and I was a *psychic medium*!

Now, some of you may think I was a bit slow on the uptake and I can tell you now, so do I. After that television program, my mind started racing at a million miles an hour. Hungry for more information, I went to the bookcase and rummaged for a book I remembered a friend had given me ages ago. It was called *The Eagle and The Rose* by Rosemary Althea, an American medium who claims to have a native American named 'Eagle Feather' as her main guide. That book had sat on the shelf for ages – I'd accepted it from my friend to be polite, because I really couldn't see at the time what a New Age American's experiences would possibly have to do with my life! Now I began to read. Page after page, the author's experiences parallelled my own. As Althea described her journey into recognising and identifying her guides, shivers ran uncontrollably through me. The changing faces on the wall, the comments about everyday things, it was all there.

I read that book in record time and then went to the library. I found a book called *Voices in My Ear* by Doris Stokes and a few other on clairvoyance. I fell in love with Doris Stokes, especially her dedication to the parents of lost children. I went out and bought *Crossing Over* and *One Last Time* by John Edward. I read and read, day in and day out. I swallowed the words right off the pages. I researched as much as I could. Book after book confirmed over and over that what I was seeing and hearing was, in fact, the spirit world. Finally, everything truly made sense. With the dawning of that realisation came a huge tidal wave of relief. My mind's frantic search for explanations, the hunt for military spies and space aliens, the terrible fear that I was losing my grip on sanity, all were instantly and forever swept away. I was a channel for spirit – a *medium* – it was as simple as that.

I quickly realised I had another problem. How do you convince your family that you are in contact with the spirit world? My mum was pretty sceptical, to say the least. One day I am telling her that army guys are hunting me down, and the next I'm convinced I am a psychic medium? I had to convince my family and myself, but how? I needed proof and fast. My mum and family thought I was madder than ever. You have to remember how much I had already put them through. I had involved my mum in all my problems. First with Crystal going, my boys being taken away from me, followed by the nervous breakdown, then the voices and people in the backyard. I think my mum had really had enough of me by this stage. Not to mention the alcohol ever present in my life causing destruction whenever I opened another bottle. How do you convince people who have known you your entire life that you are suddenly psychic?

The opportunity came one day during a phone call. My grandfather came through, clear as a bell, while I was having a chat with mum.

"Remind her about the Cherry Ripe packets," Grandpop instructed me.

Now, I did not have a clue what he was on about. When I relayed the message to Mum, I heard a little exclamation of surprise on the other end of the phone.

"When Grandpop was in hospital," Mum explained, "he wasn't allowed to eat high-fat foods. He used to smuggle in Cherry Ripe chocolates and I would smuggle the empty wrappers out for him when I came to visit."

I listened to Mum's story with a smile – no doubt about Grandpop!

"After Grandpop died," Mum continued, "they found a heap of empty Cherry Ripe packets in his trousers."

It wasn't something Mum had ever mentioned to anyone. A little later, I told mum about a portable record player my grandmother had – my grandmother had died when I was four years old. She began to believe after that.

Now that the penny had truly dropped, the advanced training could begin. I understood that when I had 'read' people at the supermarket or while working at the shop, I wasn't tuning into their thoughts but I was in fact tuning into the spirit world. There I was, thinking I was reading minds but in fact I was tuning into the relatives around them! The guides started to teach me how to identify who was who around a person. I learned to identify their gender and status. One side of the person belonged to the mother's side and the other the spouse's and father's side. I adopted John Edward's way of identifying children from parents and grandparents. In *One Last Time*, John Edward notes that for him, spirits appear around a client in the same pattern as a family tree. The mother's side was on the left, the father's side on the right, grandparents above and children below. I applied his approach to my own readings and it seemed the spirit world was happy to do this with me as well. The only exception in my readings is the odd father who will appear on the mother's side, usually when mum is still with us in life. It became easier each time to identify the relationship of the spirit to the client.

Next, I had to learn about clairvoyance. Clairvoyance, to me, is like a memory. In the same way that you might picture your bedroom or workplace in your mind, I see messages from the spirit world. I see symbols and pictures in my mind and by interpreting these symbols, I am able to relay the message. I am very clairaudient (hearing things psychically) and clairsentient (sensing/feeling things psychically) but clairvoyance (seeing things psychically) is something that is always developing for me. It's as though I have a dictionary of pictures in my mind. These pictures can be as simple as a man holding a badge. Now, that can be interpreted as anything from a military man to a policeman. A large ship can mean that a man fought overseas in the war, any war. Or it can be interpreted in a different way, perhaps to indicate that the spirit migrated to Australia. A man with a skipper's cap on can indicate several things. It can mean that the man was in the armed forces and loved the water or that he was in the Navy, had a love for the water and spent many hours at sea. As I gain experience in my work, certain images have come to have a very specific meaning and of course the dictionary is being added to all the time.

Usually, there's a degree of all three skills at work when I receive a message from spirit. I can hear a voice, see an image, and feel with my body the gist of what is being communicated through me. As you may imagine, this can be very confusing and it takes considerable concentration to keep all the receptors open at the same time. Concentrating too hard can interrupt the process though. It is important to be open and just let the information flow without thinking - hence the "don't think" training from Peter. Being very clairaudient, I tend to rely on what I heard, at the expense of information that came through in other ways, but over time I've improved. Trial and error and a persistent and loving guide will always be the best teachers.

As I mentioned before, my guides spent a lot of time teaching me to 'listen' with every part of my body from my head to my toes. I know that sounds strange but this is true clairsentience. A blind man once told me that it's the same when you have no sight. The blind must 'listen' with their whole body. A good way to practice this skill is to blindfold yourself and see what you can 'hear' with your feelings as well as your ears. It takes a lot of practice, but it's a skill I believe everyone is capable of developing.

To conduct a reading, I reach into a person's aura and 'listen' with my whole body. I believe that the spirit world operates on a different frequency than we do, and as a medium I am able to tune into this frequency. It's like the difference between AM and FM radio. By extending my aura, I am able to tap into this special frequency and invite the spirit world a little closer to me. The other senses then come into play. The hardest part is in the interpretation. Of course, there's some degree of interpretation as the medium translates a visual image into words, but ultimately, I feel it's best just to say what you see, feel and hear without trying to make sense of it. The client will usually be able to understand immediately what might seem a little ridiculous to the medium! For example, Nanna might come through for a client and try to validate her presence by mentioning the green monkey tattoo she had on her bum! If I don't relay "spirit is showing me a green monkey and I'm sensing this has something to do with a bottom" to the client because it sounds really silly, and a very specific and personal validation has missed its mark. Both Nanna and the client miss out because the medium has interpreted the signs as silly. As I have said many times, I am just the postman – it's not my job to read the mail but just to deliver it!

Being a good medium involves many factors such as diet, exercise and rest. I have learned that my menstrual cycle can play havoc with my abilities. If I don't eat properly, I will quickly run out of energy during readings. I can't drink alcohol or do anything that may harm my body. I really don't even like to take paracetamol or other everyday medicines if it can be avoided. This is because the spirit world likes a nice clear vessel to work through. Some mediums might drink and smoke, but I feel that I must respect my body, especially after my not-so-pure past! I am now a vegetarian and make sure that my iron and protein levels are top notch. Rest is perhaps one of the most important things to honour. I've come to know my limits and I don't overstep them. For me, being a medium has meant a complete life change, and one that I have had to pursue with diligence to be successful. I never make the mistake of thinking that I can't improve further as there's always so much more to learn. After the best readings and the not so great ones, I tell myself that I am learning all the time. I understand that the training never really ends.

After about six months of the advanced training, I decided to put my skills to the test and advertise for the first time. I received three responses to my ad in the Sunday newspaper. One was from a woman named Angela, who lived a fair distance away, another was from a fellow who ended up having a phone reading, and the third from a woman whom I saw personally. This client lived about an hour from me and had lost her brother due to suicide only five weeks prior to the reading. In my eagerness to help her, my inexperience quickly became very obvious to me. Spirit gave details regarding the motive for the suicide, which opened a huge can of worms for that family. In my quest to give accurate and specific information, I unwittingly caused problems for the grieving family. That was something I hadn't bargained for and certainly something I never wanted to repeat. Despite my inexperience, the reading was very accurate and I went on to read for other members of that family. Still, those readings were a cautionary experience from which I learned some very valuable lessons.

Nowadays, I will never attempt to give reasons for suicide no matter how clearly they come through to me from the spirit world. That's not my job. To my mind, a medium is not a soul-saver, a detective, a psychologist or a settler of property disputes after someone dies. A medium is certainly not there to analyse why someone killed themselves as I very quickly learned. I see it as my job to validate the existence of spirit and that is all. I also have rules about the time that should elapse after the loss and before clients can come to me for a reading. It varies, but I have one hard and fast rule regarding this: parents who have lost a child cannot have a reading less than six months after the loss. From experience, I have learned that acceptance takes at least that long – often longer. As a medium, I am always conscious of the stages involved in the grieving process. Remember, I've been there. The last thing I want to do is get in the way of healing. If clients come for a reading early, more often than not it's a way to deny what has happened and hold on. Emotions are too raw for me to be of any real help. Later, once acceptance has occurred, the reading is much more beneficial.

* * *

So the penny had finally dropped and a brand new chapter of my life had begun. At last I knew I had broken the cycle of grief in my own life and I was now on the path towards helping others do the same. In my mind, I had thoughts of appearing on television but quickly put them down to being fanciful. I even had thoughts about writing a book but berated myself for being silly. I had a *long way* to go before I could think about that sort of thing.

After the first ad, I decided to advertise locally. This was much more successful and I soon had a steady stream of clients coming to the house for readings. I gave another reading at Jimboomba, during which I was introduced to a spirit named Andre. He later popped up again in another reading for a friend of his mother. It was not long before I met his mum, Kathy, and spent two weekends doing readings on the Sunshine Coast through my connection with her. Word began to spread and I took up travelling to give readings at people's homes. It seemed to work out quite well. I drove hundreds of kilometres in those early days!

I was still working at the airforce base and one day, one of the women there asked if I would be interested in doing a talk for her meditation group. This would be my first group reading and needless to say, I was very nervous! The spirits didn't let me down though. They came through so strongly one after the other, there was a moment that I realised I was doing the same thing as John Edward. I thoroughly enjoyed every minute of it. At this reading, I met a woman named Glynn with whom I immediately 'clicked'. She later mentioned our meeting to a woman named Janet Gibson who insisted on meeting me. At the time, Janet said that she heard my name and knew she had to meet me. Little did I realise the role that Janet would play in my life. I liked her so much and she had so much knowledge. It was funny because she stayed for about two hours. I ended up asking *her* a lot of questions that I needed answers to. She answered them so well that I felt I couldn't charge her at all, but Janet insisted on paying a part fee. When she left, I remember putting her name into my mobile phone. At the time, I wasn't sure why I did that, I just did. Unknown to me, spirit had just presented me with my first human guide!

Soon afterwards, I received another phone call from a woman requesting a group reading. Word was really spreading fast! I decided I needed business cards and proudly added 'Group Readings' to my list of services. When I saw an advertisement for a psychic fair, I thought 'why not?' I asked my guides if I should call to find out more. There was no negative reply, so I did. I was hired for the Caboolture show on the 15th and 16th of February 2003. Things were moving fast for me as a professional medium. It was all *very* exciting.

Chapter 10

Special Readings, Special Friends

I was in the toilet not long before the Caboolture show, when I suddenly felt a presence in the room. The spirit world has no sense of decorum! I kept hearing the name 'Angela' and finally remembered the lady who had answered my very first ad but was living a long distance away. I had kept her number, so I called her and we finally met at the fair. The hall was crowded. I was in the middle of another reading when I heard someone say "Look up!" I looked up and saw a woman with long brown hair and then heard the name Angie. I also heard a *Guns and Roses* song playing in my head. Shortly afterwards when Angela sat before me for her reading, her husband Warren came through. It was a beautiful reading and one I will never forget. I will let Angela recount her part of the story:

Angie's Story

When my husband, Warren, passed away, I was so devastated. We had been friends for a long time before falling in love and moving in together. Life for us as a couple was extremely happy. We were very much in love and the best of mates, rarely did an angry word pass between us. Warren became a wonderful stepfather to my three children and along came baby, Cherish. Soon after she was born, we were able to buy our own home and life for us was perfect.

Not long after moving in and starting to plan our renovations, Warren became ill and jaundiced. Subsequent tests proved that he was experiencing liver failure and would require a transplant. After only nine months in our new home and six weeks in hospital, Warren passed away due to acute liver failure and septicaemia. He was thirty-six years old. Cherish was just two. I was totally overwhelmed by grief and very frightened. I knew a long, dark road lay ahead for me as I had already lost my father and a best friend. I did not know if I had the strength to go through the whole grieving process when I had loved Warren as much as I did.

I consider myself to be very lucky to be a very spiritual person and I am a firm believer in life after death. I remembered that there were mediums and I began to look through the newspapers. I saw Charmaine's ad and gave her a call just to enquire. She took my phone number, saying she would give me a call when next in my area. A few months later, I was having a particularly low day when Charmaine called to let me know that she would be doing readings in a nearby hall on the following Saturday.

She said a male spirit with the initial 'W' had come into the toilet, saying the name 'Angie' over and over. Warren had urged Charmaine to ring me, knowing that I would be able to attend. I smiled my first genuine smile in a long time, knowing that was something the Warren I knew would do, be cheeky enough and forward enough to arrange a meeting from the other side.

I arrived at the hall with mixed emotions; I was so excited that I was going to be hearing from Warren, yet saddened too that it could not be in the way we used to talk, face to face. And what if Charmaine was not genuine? If it was only a fluke when she had rang me? My mind was soon put at ease though when I sat down opposite Charmaine and she already knew who I was as Warren had pointed me out and blared the *Guns 'n 'Roses* song *Patience* to her, which was a favourite of ours. He went on to describe himself, how he passed, his car and many personal details about both my life and his. He commented on what the kids had been up to and how he says goodnight to Cherish when she goes to bed. He talked about how he liked the blues and yellows I had been painting all week in the playroom for the kids. He told me how much he loves me and how "you are the most beautiful woman on the planet". He still melted my heart as he always did.

By the end of the reading, I knew without a doubt that Charmaine had brought through Warren, and between Charmaine, Warren and myself there was not a dry eye in the house. Charmaine was as moved as I was, as it was a very emotional experience and the healing was just so strong. Warren really is such a beautiful and caring spirit. I went home feeling a lot lighter as I knew for sure that he was ok and had made it to the spirit world.

Charmaine and I have since become friends and Warren has interrupted our conversation many times! He has come through strongly at every opportunity to show his love and support and to prove his existence on the other side. It is very comforting. I believe if everyone could have this experience with a genuine medium, it would go a long way toward alleviating those very painful, very dark days of the grieving process.

At one reading Warren even brought through information about another man who would soon be sharing my life. I am now very much in love with a wonderful man who makes me very happy, and I know that Warren approves! As I write this, I remember back to one reading where Warren commented, "You don't notice the birds or the frogs anymore". He was referring to the fact that through my grief I had 'lost my spark' and said this made him sad.

I imagine how much he would now be smiling as he watches Jon and I admiring the redwing parrots on our birdfeeder, and how much I adore the little green frogs on the kitchen window as I wash the dishes at night.

Because of this healing, I know that Warren and I are both free to be happy.

The Caboolture show was a great success and from there, the word just kept on spreading. I was hired for private readings, group readings and more psychic fairs including one in Beaudesert. My next lot of business cards had 'psychic fairs' added to the list. At the psychic fair in Beaudesert, I was reading for a lady whose grandmother had come through. About half-way through the reading, I saw my mother's pet pig, Miss Piggy. I asked the woman if her grandmother had anything to do with pigs, pets or otherwise. The client said she didn't think so, no. I felt inclined to write it down and marked the time as 3pm. Later that day, I called my mother to tell her about the show, mentioning how Miss Piggy had come through as a reference but that I could not identify why. My mother gasped. Apparently, Miss Piggy had gone on heat and had wandered off with the feral pigs. I'm sure a good time was had by all, but at about 3pm that day Mum had heard hunters shooting. With that, we assumed poor Miss Piggy had come to say goodbye.

The Beaudesert show had taught me something important about my physical condition during a reading. It seemed that my wires became crossed when I tried to conduct readings during the heavier times of menstruation and I would have no choice but to cease the readings for the day. I remember having to apologise at the Beaudesert show after lunch on the Sunday for this reason. My wires were really crossed and I suspected word of mouth would be pretty awful after such a lousy day. If only I had the answer to this problem! It was frustrating to fight against your own natural hormones and have no idea what to do. If only I had another medium to talk to, that would be nice. Most other readers at the show read the cards and did not attempt medium work and I was a little daunted at the prospect of asking them about their cycle as I barely knew them. Mediums work differently to card readers and have to depend on all of their senses to get results. Perhaps it's not the same for all female mediums, but I know now to honour that time and rest for a day or two.

I was learning so much from just going out and doing the work. It was not just about my skills as a medium, it was about the spirits, the clients and the universe as a whole. There was so much to learn on so many levels. I had to learn about the ethics of mediumship, the techniques of good presentation and of course continue developing my skills for the actual reading process. The information was coming in at an amazing speed at this point. Not all spirits communicated in the same manner and sometimes what I thought was one thing could end up being something else. The real skill is in the interpretation and this is where things go wrong. A boat can mean war, a love for fishing, an overseas holiday or simply a boat. Being the perfectionist I am, I wanted to get it right. This was frustrating at times and left me feeling very much like I wanted to go back to a life where you just did your job and went home, a job where hearts and souls were not aching to be healed - a job where I would probably be bored out of my mind. I pushed on and when great results did come, they were so very rewarding that it made up for the days when things were a little haywire. I was learning all the time and my personality expects that I should know it all – yesterday, if possible. Because of this, one of my greatest lessons was to learn patience.

"Patience, Charmaine, slow down!" Peter told me over and over. I did as he said, sometimes with surprising results, but patience was never my strong point and to this day, my impatience can get in the way of accuracy at times. One person I truly admired was Doris Stokes and I really wanted to reach her level of accuracy. I once spent weeks just asking my guides to give me names and I would then try to get them. It was usually successful, but sometimes in a reading a name would not come at all. Patience. I really wanted to show them patience. I found this particularly hard when I was tired. Yes, patience and pacing seemed to be the keys to bringing through the clearest information. I could have screamed with impatience some days and I still feel that way at times. I just had this overwhelming desire to give every possible little detail to the clients sitting there in front of me utterly consumed by grief. Of course, no one could give them what they really wanted, but it was important for me that I give the best I was capable of.

Despite the problems at Beaudesert, I was receiving calls left right and centre, and because I was prepared to travel, I was able to do lots of great readings. I was still on a rapid learning curve too – I was learning about the Big Things - forgiveness, controlling anger and especially, patience. I was learning so much about compassion and understanding, it had a very strong healing effect on me. It was clear that the sadness in my own life provided invaluable experience for conducting readings and making my clients comfortable. I found I was able to empathise with them because I knew how it felt to lose a child, a brother or a father, not to mention friends and grandparents. Perhaps more importantly, I knew how it felt to lose oneself while trapped in a cycle of grief. I had personally walked the path and had fallen into so many potholes along the way, I realised I had many valuable insights to share. Most of my sessions would end in talks about coping strategies, and I feel *this* is the real work.

It was about this time that I felt compelled to advertise in the place I used to live, Stanthorpe. This was the place where everything had gone wrong for me; the place I lost my boys and where no one cared or even tried to understand me. Except for my mum who still lived there, there was no one I wished to even associate with. The town really had left its mark on me and I dreaded the idea of ever setting foot there again. Despite all these negative feelings, I felt such a strong pull to advertise and do some readings there. In March I advertised in the local newspaper as an experienced medium. I received eight calls in all.

Mandy was the first person to call me that day. When she walked into the room for her reading, Mandy looked very thin and very stressed. I could feel her pain as she stepped through the door. She wore it like a heavy cloak. It was a pain I could immediately identify, for walking by her side was the spirit of a young girl. She was such a strong young spirit and I was able to describe her features to a tee. The spirit said that her name began with a T, and that was the first time I met Tash. As I spoke, that heavy cloak began to slip from Mandy's shoulders. I understood then why I had felt so driven to return to Stanthorpe. This poor woman and her beautiful daughter were the reason I had to come back to this hell town, and I for one was glad I had made the effort. Mandy was beside herself with grief and it felt like I was looking at myself seventeen years ago when I had lost Crystal. This was one reading that I needed to do as perfectly as my skills would allow me. It was successful with all relevant facts coming through beautifully. Mandy left that day a changed woman and her story is a tale filled with tears, strength and inspiration. She kindly recounts her story here in her own words:

Natasha -"My Angel"

1/4/92 – 14/12/2002

Friday 13th December 2002

I had been getting migraines all week, so Mum had to come shopping with me in Warwick to help look after Nicolas and Natasha. Mum took the kids Christmas shopping and spoilt Natasha rotten. I told her not to ask for too much, to which she replied, "Don't worry Mum, Nan loves spoiling me!" (Not really the point.) When we got home, Tasha wrapped all the presents for every one and then took off outside to play with her brother. Being the first day of school holidays, there was plenty to do. They were two peas in a pod. My friend Glenda always said they were attached at the hip. How Natasha carried him around I have no idea.

Saturday 14th December 2002

I was having a sleep-in because of the headaches I had been having. Natasha brought in a cup of tea for me which I thought was really strange because she only did that for me on Mothers' Day. When I woke up again there was a bunch of roses that she and her little brother Nic had picked for me with a note saying, "To a very special mummy, Love from Tash and Nic".

At about 10 o'clock, I had started vacuuming when Tasha yelled out that she was going for a ride on her bike. I told her not to be too long. She said she wouldn't be and added "I love you Mummy". This was a normal thing for her. She was always going to look for crystals at the neighbour's place. She was a very bush-wise kid and always careful.

Charmaine Wilson

I had a really strange feeling in the pit of my stomach for most of the morning. It occurred to me about lunch time that I hadn't seen her for a while but still it didn't worry me because the neighbours were camping on the block, so I assumed she was down there with them. I couldn't eat any lunch.

I had to go and pick up my eldest son up at 3 pm that afternoon when he had finished work. My husband was in the shed, so I knew Tash would be alright when she came home. I said to my sister that when Tash got home (still not thinking anything had happened to her) I was going to get cranky with her because she was supposed to clean her room, which I had ended up doing for her anyway.

We were getting ready for a Christmas party and I told Kyle to go down and get her so she could get ready. When he got back, he told me that they had not seen her all day. I started crying. My husband told me she was going to be alright, but we were both freaking out. We looked everywhere that we thought she might have been. We found her bike and clothes near the dam. Her father came back with Nic after searching - the rest is just a blur.

At about 6 pm that night, I called my brother and dad to help us look for her and rang the police about 6.30 pm. There were many people at the house trying to help us look for her. Just going through the efforts of trying to stay calm for the rest of the family was really hard. I was thinking I had to be strong for them. This time was the very hardest, not really knowing where one of my kids was and thinking some really horrible thoughts as to what had happened to her. The police were very kind and told us to get some sleep, but sleep was not an option. I don't think I could have if I tried.

We had to wait until 10am Sunday morning for the police divers to come from Brisbane before we found her in the dam, right next to the shed. We were told that she had hit her head and that she had 'dry drowned'. Even when they took her out of the dam, which I was not able to go near because they were saying it was suspicious circumstances, I still didn't believe that she had died. It wasn't until we were allowed to see her that reality hit home.

When we had found her bike near the dam, deep down in our hearts, we knew she was there but just kept hoping that we would find her safe and well. We had even sent our son into that dam to look for her. I thank God that he didn't go.

I still couldn't believe that she had drowned; she had won plenty of medals at school for swimming and was such a strong swimmer.

There were so many things going through our heads, not only the loss of our only daughter but guilt for not being there. The grief was like breaking your heart into a million pieces or losing a part of your body. I think that my heart will be broken forever. Everything went by in a sort of numbing daze until the funeral, which I thought would be the hardest thing to get through. It was hard sitting there looking at that little coffin and questioning God why he would take our little girl away from us.

Charmaine

I had seen an advertisement in our local paper for a psychic medium who was coming to town. I was thinking about going to see her but I kept putting off the phone call. I suppose I didn't really know what I was going to be told. I finally rang and made an appointment with Charmaine.

I really needed to know whether my little one was alright and that she wasn't scared and cold. Most of all, I wanted to know what had happened to her. As I walked into the room and sat down, Charmaine said that I had a young female spirit with me and that she was a lot younger than me. It took about a minute for her to tell me that it was my daughter. Charmaine told me that her name started with 'T,' and that it was a nickname. Charmaine had got her name - Tasha. She went on to tell me what had happened to Tash that day at the dam and even mentioned the bump on her head from hitting something in the water.

At that stage, I cried. I just couldn't believe that she would get anything about Natasha at all. Charmaine then told me a lot more about what had happened to her and that it wasn't my fault, it was her time. She was able to tell me a lot about my daughter and the family. She said Tash was met by my great grandmother, and that she was alright, and that she loved us all. Charmaine was able to answer so many of my questions.

Since my daughter passed away, a lot of things have happened that I couldn't explain. Charmaine told me to ring her if there was anything I needed to ask. She has been my life-line to life. I was seeing flashes of light going past the windows when I was thinking of Tasha and finding little things that belonged to her. I would go walking and find rocks that were in the shape of hearts. Natasha told me once when we were out walking that I was hopeless at finding rocks, that's why I'm pretty sure that she had helped me find them to let me know that she was still around.

Friendship

Charmaine and I have been friends ever since that day. I feel that we share a bond. If I hadn't gone to see Charmaine, I would probably still be blaming myself for Natasha's death. I now believe we are here for our soul to keep learning life's different lessons and once we learn them, it's time to go.

It is still really hard to cope at times and I will miss Natasha every day of my life, but knowing she is still around in a different form has lessened the heartache a little. With my belief in heaven and destiny or fate, whatever you call it, and Charmaine's help, I believe it has saved me from losing my grip on life and from going insane. I really hope that my story can help in a little way. My advice to anyone is to keep an open mind when someone passes over.

After Mandy's reading, I decided I would like to do more for people in such deep grief. I offered Mandy further help by giving her my home number and asking her to call, even if she just needed to talk. I follow through and ring clients occasionally, just to see how they are coping. I think back on all those times when I was grieving and had nobody to talk to. If I could be that somebody for someone like Mandy, then I was only too happy to do it. Naturally, there is no money involved. Anyone who says medium work is just a scam to take money off the grieving has either not had the need for a medium reading or has not come across a genuine reader. I have seen the benefits with my own eyes. Medium work is all about helping those of us left behind to accept our loved ones in a new form, not taking anything away from them. Genuine mediums offer a gift to the bereaved that no one else can give.

Anyone who has lost someone very close will agree that it is a life-changing experience to receive messages from their loved ones. It can be a huge comfort knowing they are still around. I know that at the time I lost Crystal, I would have given every cent I had just to know she was ok. That is what I feel the sceptics are missing. I'm sure many sceptics have experienced the pain of grief and sincerely hope that they are at peace with the loss. Wouldn't it be nice for them though to give something a go rather than loudly (and intrusively) declaring every medium to be a fake? I'm not naïve enough to suggest that all mediums are altruistic at heart, and I know not all people practicing as mediums are true mediums. When sceptics constantly declare that all mediums are frauds because communication with the afterlife is impossible, many grieving people take notice and are denied an opportunity to experience the specific kind of comfort a genuine medium can provide. To me that seems such a narrow-minded and selfish position to take.

Chapter 11

Girl in a Million

It's The Military, Man!

He's in camouflage, he's a military man,
hiding a little boy deep within.
He is dressed in green, brown and fawn,
waiting for a war to dawn.
He packs an M16 and a hand grenade,
He's got everything, he's a highly trained killing mac
hine.
He's in the air force, the army and the navy
Patrolling the sky, the land and the sea,
A soldier, a warrior, a fighter times three,
That's the military man.!

He's protecting his country,
he's protecting his freedom
Protecting the children and all the pretty women.
He's fighting for his rights, his freedom of choice,
fighting in a language called the military choice.
His life's is not his own,
He will be leaving his family, leaving his home.
That's the military man.

He's an ambassador of peace.
A paid hit man.
He does what he's told,
he is under command Protecting our country,
our great wide land; That's the military man!

He will be leaving the beaches, he'll be leaving the sun
Leaving his lazy afternoons of fun,
Lest we forget the diggers gone by
 It makes me question and wonder why
Do we have to fight, does it have to continue?
Is there anything that we can do to save our military
man?

Cause they are fighting a war that is not our own,
won't you leave our boys alone?
Fight your own war, send them home
Cause we really love our military men!

In April of 2004, I heard of a psychic artist living close to my mum. I have always been fascinated by psychic art and was keen to see the process in action. I made appointments for mum and myself. The reading was thorough and the picture was remarkable. Many things made sense as the picture developed. When the artist drew a tunnel with a digger at the end, I immediately interpreted it to mean that I would start doing more readings at the RSL clubs around my area. I had been feeling this for a while and the drawing confirmed I was on the right track. My grandfather had been a veteran. He was in the Light Horse regiment during World War II (although from what I understand, the regiment rode motorbikes by then, instead of horses). The digger in the picture had a feather in his hat, so maybe the message was down to Grandpop, but for me the meaning was clear. Somehow I would be doing more group readings in connection with the RSL. I just knew it.

As a rule, I don't have readings from psychics much these days, but that one confirmed what spirit had been whispering to me for some time. The trouble with being a psychic and getting a reading is that you tend to interpret also. Although I usually have a fair idea as to what is happening in my life and that the directions I am taking are correct, it can still be nice to have double confirmation. Good readers have brought up the most embarrassing things for me sometimes. I vividly remember meeting another medium who offered me a reading in 2004. Naturally, my brother Martin decided to get in on the act. In serious tones, the medium informed me that my brother seemed to be coming through. To my complete horror, the only thing she could get besides the details of his death was one word: 'snot'! Obviously, Martin still had the market cornered on being bad. I nearly fell through the floor with embarrassment as the memories came flooding back. Needless to say, I didn't explain to the medium the significance of my dear departed brother's message of love.

The day after the reading with the psychic artist, a woman named Donna called me. She explained she was a representative of the *RSL Girl in a Million Quest*. The Quest is run by RSL clubs in Queensland each year. Single girls over the age of 18 have a chance to win wonderful prizes whilst learning more about our heritage and raising funds to enhance the quality of retired veterans' lives. Donna asked if I would be interested in participating in a joint fundraiser for the retired vets. I had tingles running all through my body and did not hesitate to accept. Wow! The drawing flashed into my mind and somehow I knew that this was going to be bigger than even I could imagine. To this day, that picture hangs on the wall in my office.

A recent group reading I had held at Ipswich had drawn the attention of the local press and I was about to go up the coast and out west to RSL Clubs and other venues. The idea of raising funds for retired veterans really appealed to me. You see, even though I am not an advocate of war, I still believe that military men and women past and present have done a great job. I really loved the idea that I might be able to help the old men and women who had made our country safe many years ago by giving something back. I made an arrangement with Donna concerning fees and we set the date of June 4th for the first ever *Girl in a Million/Spirit Whispers* joint fundraising event.

The groups went well, with those in Gympie, Dalby and Bundaberg going exceptionally well. I had another function in Ipswich, which was my biggest yet and also one of my best. It seemed that the spirit world was warming up to the idea of group readings and I was enjoying myself to the max. My biggest number had been about 40, but I was happy with this as I was able to correctly identify where the energies were coming from. It seemed like I had gone up in stages - from 10 to 20 to 30 to 40.

My guides had not let me down to this point and were still teaching and guiding me at a pace that would not overwhelm me.

The first read for *The Girl in a Million* was a real success. Fifty people had attended the function and many received excellent validations from spirit. It was pretty clear that even those who hadn't made a direct connection were deeply moved and uplifted by the experience. Donna was very impressed by the response, realising quickly that as a team we could not only raise substantial funds for veterans, but we could also heal broken hearts along the way! She went home and sent an email to all the other entrants and fundraising coordinators in Queensland to let them know. Before long, I had been booked for *Girl in a Million* functions in Ayr, Burleigh Heads, Gatton, Greenbank, Nerang and Ipswich as well as at clubs in Bundaberg, Mackay, Rockhampton, Gympie and Dalby.

Donna and I were working very well as a team and decided to try and drum up some media coverage for the shows. Donna contacted radio and television stations via email about the work we were planning. The following Monday, I received a call from Channel Nine's *Brisbane Extra* program and radio station B105, asking if I would be willing to be interviewed on air and perhaps give a demonstration of my work. Brisbane Extra went to air at 5.30pm Monday to Friday before the daily news, and B105 were actually looking for a resident psychic. Well, I was ecstatic!

The television show wanted to shoot the reading the following Friday. I had to arrange a venue close to the television station and also a crowd to participate in a group reading – in three days. Fortunately, friends owned a restaurant close by and they were more than happy to let me use it for the day. I made three phone calls and asked for people who had preferably not had a reading with me to be rounded up, and lo and behold, we had a crowd.

As with all things to do with spirit, it just fell into place.

I was so nervous leading up to the television shoot, that I rescheduled my Thursday appointments. On the one hand, I was on a real high – my first television appearance. On the other hand, I was panicking that spirit would get camera shy and I'd wind up looking like a complete idiot. I was up and down like a yoyo – a real mess. On the Sunday following the first *Girl in a Million*, I had a minor car accident and this prompted me to get an office. To add to the stress levels, Friday morning seemed to be the only convenient time for the furniture men to deliver my office furniture and for someone to come and connect the electricity. Somehow, I understood that this was my guides' way of keeping my feet planted firmly on the ground.

When I arrived at the restaurant, there was a crowd of about forty people. Some I knew and some I didn't, but one thing we all had in common was that we were very nervous.

The shoot was an experience I will never forget. I think my heart was the loudest I have ever heard it and my top kept gaping open for the entire world to see. Now, I am not big-busted but had worn my push-up bra to maximise my gorgeousness for telly. I ended up spending way too much time trying to prevent the viewers from seeing their first topless medium! Needless to say, I was uncomfortable and to make matters worse, the first lady I read seemed to have developed psychic amnesia.

"I feel you have a male around you whose name begins with the letter A," I said, in my best television voice.

"No" the woman responded flatly. From behind her, the woman's friend whispered, "What about your husband, Andy?" Well, talk about a tough crowd!

Later, the woman admitted to me that in fact all I had said made sense to her - she just had a bit of stage-fright. After the second reading, I began to feel a little better and by the fourth reading, we had a really good flow going.

After the restaurant shoot, a mother/daughter team and myself went to the local cemetery to do a private reading, just for the atmosphere. This went extremely well. All in all, I was very happy with the day but was glad to see the end of it. It was a great relief to rip off that damn push-up bra and put my feet up after a very tiring day.

Brisbane Extra told me the piece would go to air on the following Wednesday but somehow I knew it would be the Tuesday, so I cancelled my appointments for that afternoon. Sure enough, it went to air on the Tuesday. Along with all the show's regular viewers, I watched myself on television for the very first time. It was a great show in actual fact. The station had done my life's passion justice. Current affairs programs have a reputation for 'trashing' psychics, but this show treated what I was doing with respect. Although my nerves were apparent (as were my magnificently uplifted bosoms!), spirit had let me shine on screen. The segment portrayed psychic work in a very positive light. As usual, I thanked spirit because I feel that they are the ones that pull the strings after all. They even put me in the same light as my favourite psychic, John Edward, and that was like icing on the cake! I learned a lot from the experience, including the fact that TV really does add 10 pounds!

After the show aired, the phone rang at a slow but steady pace. As I have said before, my guides are constantly monitoring how much I can handle and adjusting the flow accordingly. We had a function planned for Burleigh Heads on the 12th of August and another at Gatton on the 13th. The Burleigh show was the biggest yet - 73 people in all and an excellent one. Everything flowed so well. I was ecstatic. The coordinator booked another show immediately. People had come from all over the south-east because of the television show. I left Burleigh feeling very optimistic about the Gatton show.

I would love to be able to tell you that Gatton was a huge success, but unfortunately it wasn't. When I woke up that day, I had a feeling I could not shake. I looked at the kitchen clock a little later and saw it was 9:11 am. Those numbers – 9.11 - always made me feel uneasy. I looked at my phone a bit later on, and lo and behold: 9:11am. Bugger!

A few minutes later and there it was again, 9:11am on the bedroom clock. It seemed that all my clocks were out of sync in time terms but exactly in sync with the 9:11 message that gave me the heebie-jeebies. I frantically asked my guides if this was an omen and they said, "You will be reading fine." Well, that was ok then. I should have felt relieved, but as the day carried on, I could not shake my bad mood. We arrived at the venue and were told we had to wait until the *Last Post* had played, so we started about five minutes late. That was ok.

Deep into the life of Winnie, the reading is interrupted by the blare of the club loudspeaker. A loud crunching noise followed by: "Ticket 772, Dorothy Smith." Oh no!

It seemed spirit would have to wait until the raffles had been drawn. I was informed that the draw had to take place immediately and the speakers could not be turned off as some patrons were in the other part of the room. I tried to continue as numbers and names were called, but after ten minutes, I surrendered and called an unscheduled interval. Ten minutes later, the audience returned but by then the members' draw was up to $4000 and the club had to keep drawing (and broadcasting) until a winner could be found.

Well! After what seemed like forever, the announcements stopped. I resumed reading – with a huge sigh of relief – the instant the Chook Wheel clickety-clicked into life. Donna begged the manager to please stop the draw until the end of the reading. This nearly caused a punch up at the front bar. I don't know what the universe was on about that night, maybe the Friday 13th thing, but unbelievably the members' draw did not go off till 11.20pm. We were walking out the door as the winner's name was announced.

* * *

The following Monday was a little bizarre. I had four readings scheduled. The first one went very well. The second was an excellent reading with a lady who had driven from Gympie. Towards the end of the reading, I had this 'A' come in. I thought it might have been an Arthur. No, there were no 'A' the lady told me. What was strange was the fact that the A seemed to be getting stronger. The next reading was a little late and I immediately got a Dorothy, a Helen, an Emily and a Jean. No to all, except the Jean. I could not understand it - they were so clear. Nothing but names came through. I went for a walk to see if I could uncross my wires. I returned to my client, apologised for the delay and resumed the reading. I was relieved when the client received validations from 'Caroline'. Then the A came back. Arthur was definitely the name.

As soon as the next client sat down, I was seeing a golf course and then a wedding. 'Yes' to both. Then her mother Jean came through, followed by Dorothy, who acknowledged her daughter Helen and then the grandmother, Emily. They must have been a bit early when they came through before. It never ceases to amaze me when spirits turn up early and come into another reading. Before long, in came the A again. Arthur - I was very clear on that.

I was doing the grocery shopping after that reading when I got a phone call. The second lady, the one from Gympie, called to tell me some bad news. When she had arrived home, her mother had called to tell her that Uncle Arthur had died that morning - while the reading with me was in progress! Poor old Uncle Arthur! He just sat with me all day announcing his arrival in Heaven. I can just see it. While we were talking to her father, Bill, he must have said to me, "Arthur's just turned up." The mind boggles. I wonder what he must have thought, coming straight from his deathbed to a psychic medium's room in Ipswich and then not to be claimed! Poor old Uncle Arthur.

In actual fact, this has happened a few times. Occasionally, the names and details I am picking up actually belong to the next reading. When this happens, I'm reminded of a scene in the movie "Ghost" where Whoopi Goldberg's character has all the spirits waiting in the room with her whilst the clients wait outside in the waiting room for their turn. In my mind's eye, I can almost hear and see the spirits saying, "Well, if this lot's not going to talk, *I* have something to say." Before shows, I distinctly get the impression of having a big line of spirits that had been following me all day, and honestly some of them get so close that I find myself gasping for breath one minute and feeling like I am having a heart attack the next. I can almost see a conga line behind me the whole day with the front spirit literally beating the others off with a stick!

Chapter 12

How Can I Help?

In November 2004, I read a book by Wayne Dyer called *There is a Spiritual Solution to every Problem*. This book was one of the most inspiring books I have ever read and for the first time, everything in my life made complete sense. In one of the chapters, Dyer writes that if you really want to make a difference in this world, you should ask the universe one question: "How can I help?" After deep thought on the chapter, I did just that, then picked up my diary. What was bothering me was the fact that people needed so much more than just a reading and I was not keen on trying to connect people over and over again. Not only did it not seem to work very well, but it was apparent to me that one reading per spirit was all anyone really needed. I mean, when life on this plane is over, there is no more information they can give you other than their name, how they died, what they were like and other personal details. When I had done multiple readings, I felt I couldn't in good conscience charge for what was essentially the same information. I picked up the diary with these thoughts in mind asking myself, "How can I help?"

A card fell out of the diary as I picked it up. I saw that it belonged to a man named Bruce Andrews. My mind went back to that bleak August day when he and his wife had entered my office. My car was blowing smoke but it seemed I was meant to get there. Despite the fact I had blown the head in the motor, I arrived on time. As I drove past my office to park, I noticed Bruce and Sharon waiting patiently at the bus stop across the road. I kept getting signs of a young child being around and the number 613 was on my mind. In fact, I had woken at precisely that time. Shortly afterwards, I met Bruce's young son, Timmy, who had been tragically killed in an accident while Bruce was driving. With their permission, their story appears below. Oh - the number 613, well Timmy was a dozer lover and his favourite dozer was a 613. I will let Sharon recount her tale here:

Tim's Story

It happened to us on the 21st of March 2004. In a split second, he was gone. We would never see him again, never be able to hear his voice, to see his smile, to watch him play outside. Our lives were changed and Tim's life taken from him. When an irresponsible 25-year-old woman ran into our vehicle, Tim was gone.

Why? Why did it have to be Tim? Why couldn't it have been one of us? Bruce and I would have gladly given our lives so that Tim could still be here. He was only 8 years old; he had so much to live for. We have searched for an answer for 11 months. We have read every book we could get our hands on, we have learned a lot but still we don't have the answer we are looking for. We were put in touch with Charmaine Wilson, a psychic medium. We didn't know what to expect but anything was worth a try.

Charmaine Wilson

We go to meet Charmaine, not having told her why we are there, or who for. We sit down; she eases us a bit, and starts to piece together why we are there. Charmaine tells us he's here, he's a child – a big kid. She tells us we didn't get to say goodbye, he passes over quickly. This is true. It happened so quickly.

We were driving along and in a split second,Tim was gone. Charmaine tells us he's rocking the baby for some reason. She says, "Is he 8-9"? Tim was 8 years old when we lost him. She asked about the letter M – is his name MIT? Bruce used to call Tim Mit and he loved it. It was special. She tells us this is an accident, a car accident, tells us not to blame ourselves. Bruce has blamed himself since it happened. He thought he didn't do enough to stop if from happening. In reality, there was nothing more he could have done, he'd got as far off the road as possible but the other car had just kept coming at us until it hit us and rolled our vehicle over.

Charmaine tells us there's not much road, sees a lot more dirt. She feels it's very quick. "Do you spin?" she asks. Tim tells her we were in a ute and we were thrown from it. Tim tells her this, so we know it's true, it is Tim. He wants us to stop blaming ourselves.

Charmaine has some trouble understanding what Tim is telling her. Why, you ask? Because he has a mouthful of pink Hubba Bubba bubble gum. We used to buy this for him, it was his favourite. Charmaine takes a sip of her diet coke and Tim kindly tells her that he drinks coke but he drinks real coke. Not that diet stuff. This is true, he was allowed to have a can of coke here and there. She tells us about Tim, what he looked like, a lot of things that she wouldn't know, she doesn't know us and she didn't know Tim. How could she know any of this? It must be true; Tim must be here telling her all of this.

He keeps rocking the baby. Charmaine doesn't understand why. It's because I am pregnant. We are expecting a baby early February 2005. Tim is trying to tell her this.

I know we are desperate to make contact with Tim, but there is nothing Charmaine tells us about him that isn't true. It is like a weight off our shoulders just to know that he is alright. In actual fact, he seems to be doing better with all this than we are. We have had three readings with Charmaine since we lost Tim, and each visit seems to get a little easier. The last two, Tim was there waiting for us to arrive.

It seems everything you say or think, Tim knows about it. He also knows this baby is a boy, true again. Tim tells us that Billy Tim will be born on 2/2/5. He likes Billy's name. His second name is in honour of Tim. We'll see when Billy is born, if Tim was right. It is so sad that he is excited about a baby brother and won't be here to have contact with him.

There is no happiness or joy to be found in death, especially the tragic taking of a child. But we can be grateful for maintaining contact with Tim through Charmaine. And also Tim can keep contact with us. To know that he is ok makes it just a little easier to try and deal with. Don't get me wrong, it has been a long hard road with more bad days than good ones.

The day we lost him, our hearts broke in two. The pain has been unbearable; we feel as if we'll never get over this. Losing someone you loved so much, for a while you can see no reason to go on.

This new baby is a blessing in disguise, a miracle, in fact. We feel that Tim has done some smooth talking with God for this baby (miracle) to be given to us.

Well, Tim told Charmaine that Billy would be born on the 2/2/5. We went into hospital on the 2/2/5 and Billy was born on the 3/2/5. Do you believe in angels? We do. We now believe that Tim will be like an angel to Billy, the little brother that he will never get to meet. We believe that he will be there watching over Billy always.

We have still not mended our hearts, we probably never will, but at least we are luckier than some; we can have a sort of contact with Tim, through Charmaine. She is truly gifted. It is all we have left, the memories we hold in our hearts.

Tim was a very special boy who is sadly missed, and always will be. But, we'd like to say *Thank You* to Charmaine, for sharing with us her special gift. Without you, Charmaine, I don't know if we'd have got through this.

IN OUR HEARTS FOREVER – TIM.

That thank you card falling out of my diary made me think, and hard. What were people looking for? What did they need? How could I help?

The number 613 and my own special numbers were circling around in my head. My own journey since my daughter's death and the trials and heartaches I had endured were foremost in my mind. My training as a medium and the ever present question asked by my many clients - Why did they die? - swirled around in my mind too. I realised that I needed to teach others how to connect and most importantly, how to understand the eternal journey of the soul. It was not enough to prove that they were in spirit and still around. I needed to teach my clients why and how to understand this for themselves. They needed to communicate on their own, without feeling the need to spend money on psychics. As with a lot of my ideas in life, this one was born with intensity from the beginning. As soon as the idea came to me, suggestions for a possible course began to tumble from the universe at such a speed that I had to write down everything quickly. Yes, I would teach my clients to understand, recognise and connect on their own. It made perfect sense. Within hours, I had a venue booked and the course outline completed. It was in this way that my seminar *Spirit Talk* was born.

What was really great was that I was able to have the venue for free. By asking for a donation from participants, I could donate the money to the community centre that worked to help the local kids to understand their lives. It was wonderful - while helping my clients - I could help some kids. I loved it and so did the centre owner, Phil. He was right behind me on this one and was keen to get it off the ground. It was arranged that we start the first six-week block in only two weeks time, so a six-week block would be completed by Christmas. As usual, the local paper got behind me and ran a story which yielded about twenty clients for the first course. I enlisted the help of my friend Val and off we went with just a skeleton of what we hoped to achieve.

The first seminar was quite successful - all twenty people claimed to get something out of it. I have since seen some of my students from that first course, and they are different people. A couple of ladies came back and did the course again when it was held two more times. They said they just enjoyed learning and reinforcing their beliefs.

Each course was a learning experience and I was able to glean a little more from each session and improve upon the previous one. It was so important for people to understand the whole life journey and the more questions I asked my guides the more often I received answers. I would dream the answers and then I would think about the dream. It was amazing the way that the answers came. I would be thinking of a question, open a book and there was the answer. My job was developing into so much more than merely giving validation of the afterlife. It included education and communication. So the seminar I now called *Spirit Talk* was up and running. I mean, why not try and teach others how to be aware, how to live in the moment and receive validation from spirit without the expense of a psychic? As 2004 drew to a close, I realised how far my work had come, and I knew the year ahead was about to open with a bang.

* * *

The Year 2004 was one I would surely remember for a long time. Sadly, it was also a year that would go down in world history because of the dreadful Christmas Tsunami.

26th of December 2004 is a date that will stay in many minds forever. That disaster of gigantic proportions was the cause of terrible grief. I wondered as I watched the shocking images on television how anyone could help those poor people who had survived. As with the September 11 terrorist attacks, I had compassion for those who had lost their lives, but it was the survivors and their grief that melted my heart. Not only had many of them lost their entire families, but their whole lives were swept out to sea. In the blink of an eye, people lost families, friends, homes, schools, jobs, places of worship, hospitals, food, water, memories - everything. That's what I call rock-bottom. In some areas, bodies were carpeting the ground in others, they had just been carried out to sea forever. It shook me very deeply to feel the sea of grief, greater than the great wave that had come from nowhere and destroyed so many lives.

The tsunami touched on one of my personal fears. I had long ago sworn off the sand and the waves, all because of a dream I had when I was a child. It seemed so real. It was of a tidal wave and it scared me because of the reality of it. I was running and running but knew it was useless. I could see people being thrown up in the foam, and it all seemed so terrifying that I woke up in a cold sweat. To this day, 32 years later, I have never forgotten the fear I felt and have only been in the surf on two occasions - once when I was dragged in and another time when I tried to body surf - tried and failed miserably, I might add! I only ever go as far as my ankles into the water, and this is no word of a lie.

The tsunami made me think that I must have lived through this fear in one of my lives.

In the first week of December, I was at Ballina and could not shake the fear of flooding. I kept hoping the floods would hold off until I got home. It had been raining a fair bit and although the locals appeared calm, I was very anxious as the waters rose visibly around us. Every part of me wanted to be safe. The tsunami brought all these fears to the surface – I imagined the terrible fear as the giant wave just kept coming and coming....

I couldn't stop crying and wished I could do more to help. I knew nothing in this world could make me go anywhere near the area because of the fear I held so deep in my soul. I was frustrated that I had no money. If I were rich, I would dig very deep and would make a difference in a material way – what real difference would my tiny donation be able to make? It was just a drop in the ocean. With each new report on television, I felt so powerless to help – I wanted to be able to soothe even one broken heart, just a little. I did what I could and I prayed for the survivors. I lit candles and sent as much healing and light as possible to the grieving. Whether it helped anyone or not, I'll never know, but it certainly helped me. Australians donated a record amount of crisis funds and supplies to the victims of the tsunami. The figures reminded me that every little bit helps, no matter how small. We don't need to be rich to make a difference in times of disaster. Sometimes it's easy to forget that if everyone just gives a dollar of loose change, it can add up to millions of dollars available for those in need. When such tragedies happen, we can all ask ourselves: "How Can I Help?" I will never forget the dreadful scenes that played daily on television that Christmas, nor will I forget the grief of those who had lost so many and so much. I only hope that time is healing them as it should.

Chapter 13

Radio Waves

At the end of 2004, I decided that I was going to tour Queensland in a big way, so I set about hiring as many function rooms and clubs as I could. I was also invited to attend the Ipswich *Girl in a Million* function to crown their Queen. Donna seated me at a table next to River 94.9 local radio morning show presenter, Ashley Mac. I was talking to him when I received the name June and a feeling of cancer. It turned out to be his mother-in-law, who had died the previous year. He was duly impressed and invited me to do a regular spot on his morning show. Ashley Mac was not keen on doing live readings on air, so we decided to get people to send in photographs via email and I would read from those. The first show was just an interview and a promotion for the show. We arranged to pre-record the first show to be aired on the 31st of January. I was hoping that the spirits would come through quickly, because I knew that I didn't have long to get them through. The radio station had given me two five-minute segments every Monday to read in. We taped each Friday. The station wanted to keep an eye on the flow and the popularity of the show.

The first reading got off to a slow start as the listener had a case of what I've come to call 'psychic amnesia'. I mention that there is a younger male that is close to her whose name begins with 'R'.

"No", she says, quite definitely. About thirty seconds later she tells me, "Oh, my Dad's name is Ray!" Little did I know that this 'psychic amnesia' would be a common ailment amongst many of my listeners.

One woman named Jenny sent a photo in. I gave her a lot of information about her mother who had passed. Jenny kept affirming everything I told her, until I got to the letter 'M' - then she said, 'No'. Strange - I seemed to have a strong connection here. A couple of days later, the same woman emailed me very apologetically to let me know that her mum's name was Mavis. Oh well, a medium gets used to this after a while.

2005 was shaping up to be a big year. The first of my live shows, now named 'Spirit Whispers', was to be held in Emerald, a small mining and cotton town in Central Queensland. The word was out and for the first time I approached the local paper with my story hoping to get some interest. I was in luck. The woman who did the interview had just lost her grandmother and was interested in seeing if she would come through. Alma came through with a force and was able to convince her grand-daughter that she was around. The young reporter was clearly impressed with the reading and reported on it favourably. Before long, I was receiving phone calls left right and centre. The Emerald show was a sell-out with 120 audience members crammed into the room. It was one of those magical shows that I have come to love.

Ben was the star of the night. He was a young spirit who had been killed in an accident and walked into the room with a slab of rum and cola cans on his shoulder and a big smile on his face. Lots of validations followed.

The big thing was that in such a small town, most of the people knew who he was. The next day, the woman I was staying with showed me a photo, and it actually freaked me out a little how well Ben had shown himself. I had been wondering why the description I gave of him had caused such a loud gasp in the room. Men as well as women left the show that night with something to think about. I immediately booked another show for August and was then inundated with requests for phone and private readings on my next visit. It was a great start of the year with the spirit world in full bloom and ready to shine.

The next show was at the Caloundra Power Boat Club. Now with my work at the radio station, I decided to ask Krista, the host of the morning show if she knew anyone in Sunshine Coast radio. She suggested that I call Hot 91 FM. Success! I was hired to appear as a guest on the Hot 91 FM breakfast show with Chrissy and Ronnie. I remembered Chrissy, as she had claimed her fame on the *Big Brother* television show in 2003. I was stoked. Chrissy had been one of my favourites on *Big Brother* and now I was the guest star on her show. The radio spot was a roaring success. The spirit world was loving being on the air waves and my phone rang about sixty times that day, as listeners called to book tickets for the Caloundra show. Once again, the show sold out.

It had been such a long day, with radio at 7:00am and the phone ringing all day non-stop. I even had to set up extra chairs just prior to the show. There I was, the 'roadie-medium', lugging chairs around the venue, when I really should have been resting and getting into 'the Zone'! I was absolutely exhausted by the time the show began and it was a big lesson for me. It was also the night

I started the *Quick Question Time* part of the show. Towards the end, I always ask if people have any questions. That first night, a woman asked me about her mum. Although this was not the usual kind of question, her mum came through very well and quickly, just like on radio. So I tried it again and it kept on working. I extended the show by a half hour to get more readings in. *Quick Question Time* was working very well, so I decided to make it a regular part of the show. It was also at this time that I decided that I could not handle the business by myself anymore. This was at the beginning of 2005 and all was going well, so I decided to ask my friend Val if she would man the phones for me so I wouldn't be so tired at the end of the day. I agreed to pay Val a small wage in return and she was happy to take the calls, but I think her family soon got sick of the constant ringing. So many people wanted private readings that I soon found myself booking motels and doing readings in locations like the Sunshine Coast and Gold Coast for three or four days at a time.

Meanwhile, the stage shows went on. The first show in Ipswich proved a roaring success. The local paper decided to put me to the test and got me to read a sceptic, a believer and a fence-sitter in one session. It was a great write-up and the show a success. The spirit world always seemed to love the shows. So many people got the message at once. The Mt Isa show was next on the list and unfortunately I discovered that what works for Brisbane will not necessarily work for Mt Isa. Although the show was a very good one, only fifteen people arrived and not all the private readings I had booked showed up. At the time, most of the people I came in contact with stated that they did not see any advertising, and had they known, they surely would have attended. The Mt Isa show proved to me beyond a doubt that I had a lot to learn in the promotion field. This life I was now living was opening doors I had never peeked in and I can tell you it was exciting. I had always fancied myself as a promotions person but in the years before my ability became apparent, had written it off due to lack of education and low self-esteem. I was now very busy but very happy in my new role as psychic medium/promotions manager.

The next show was in Nambour. This was a *Girl in A Million* function and once again, I was invited to Hot 91 to have a chat and do some on air readings with Chrissie and Ronnie.

The show sold out. It was apparent that live radio was the way to go. It was also a lot of fun. If you could have seen the expressions on Chrissie's and Ronnie's faces when I brought through a spirit, you might understand why I laughed so much on air. The goose-bumps would raise on their arms and they both looked at each other with crazy expressions, eyes wide and strange grimaces. They loved it though, and so did the listeners. So much so that they asked me to do a regular appearance. The show was to start as a regular segment and be called 'Mystic Monday'. I would be on air every second week to do readings.

After the Nambour show, I had one in Nerang and once again the numbers were small, but what an extraordinary show! The spirits that came through were mostly young, had died in extraordinary circumstances and their names were also uncannily similar. There was a Tina, Nina and Linda and a Trent, Ben and Wendy. So it was all either *in* or *en*. After this show, I was to head off on my biggest trip yet and all by myself. The North Queensland trip. It was a very gruelling schedule, but I'd never been afraid of a bit of hard work, and the tour was a total success. The shows sold out all the way up the coast, with two of the venues telling me that they could have sold twice the amount of tickets. At that point, I was happy with the numbers. Townsville had an audience of 220 and this was to be my biggest audience to date. Each club immediately rehired me to appear again in October. I was over the moon! To this point I had conducted shows of up to 120, so to see so many in the room was just a mind-blowing experience. My nerves were calm though, as message after message made the audience smile and cry all at once. It was the most amazing experience.

I was on radio on the trip up as well. It seemed my participation in radio was doing wonders for advertising. Station after station was more than happy to have me on the show to conduct readings and chat on the airwaves. On the return trip, I decided to do private readings in Rockhampton and Bundaberg. It can be quite frustrating doing private readings away from home at times, because I have found that some people just don't bother turning up. It always amazes me that they do not even think to call and cancel! I have very limited time when I am away and always have to turn people away, so it can be very unsettling when some people just don't show up. This North Queensland trip was to be my first taste of this behaviour. It was disappointing. It was a two-week journey in all, and the longest I had ever been working away from home. My phone bill was scary for that trip as it gets very lonely on the road, and as much as I appreciate this wonderful gift I have been given, I really do miss home on big trips away.

Once I returned home, I was due to start my permanent position with Hot 91. What a great day it was! Chrissie had decided to dub the show 'Two Extra Larges and a Medium'. You see, both Chrissie and Ronnie are quite well-endowed in the flesh department. Radio, oh how I love it! It is fast, exciting and the power to heal on the airwaves is phenomenal. I remember one day, a lady named Karen called the station and wanted to know if I could tell her who the spirit in her house was. The first impression I had was of a young male with some sort of head injury or illness. I was then given a 'J N/M' sound. She told me that a young male friend named Jeremy had passed due to a stroke at a very young age. I had the impression that he was in a car and was very keen on cars. Then I felt very sick. It now felt like a suicide. She told me that a friend of hers had committed suicide in his car and his name had been Greg. I gave her a few other things and thought 'well, that wasn't very much'. Next thing, a woman named Karen rings up the station, quite frantic. It seemed that it was her fiancé who had tried to connect, the one named Greg. She had been driving along the Sunshine Motorway when she heard us on the radio and had to pull over because she was crying so hard. I agreed to talk to her off-air and called her as soon as the segment had finished. When the reading began, I immediately felt the young man named Greg come back through and he gave her some further validations. Then I felt another energy.

"Have you got someone else with a 'J' name other than Jeremy? This feels like a woman"

Karen replied that she had a friend named Jodie in spirit.

"She is giving me murder or something," I told her. "I can't quite tell how she passed."

Karen told me that her friend had been killed in the Bali Bombings in 2002.

"I feel that there was another who was killed as well, who is with her."

Karen confirmed that another friend, Charmaine, had also been killed. It was strange hearing my own name. I described Jodie and Charmaine. Jodie was short-haired and sassy and Charmaine was pretty, with long, dark hair. Both were very attractive women. Jodie had just broken up with her man. Karen replied that all of this was true. It was only a short reading, but in it Jodie asked to be remembered to her brother Mark and her mum. Karen went on to tell me a very sad tale. The year after Greg's death, her good friends Jodie and Charmaine had tried to cheer her up by taking her to Bali for a holiday. Unfortunately, they had both been killed in the Bali bombs. I would love to contact Karen again to see how she is going. After her reading, I received many calls from the family of the bomb victims and later was able to connect them. Such a sad tale, but it showed me the absolute healing power of spirit and how effective radio was in getting to those who needed the validations most. I actually lived two hours from the radio station and would get up at five in the morning to make the long trek to do my one hour spot, but it was worth every minute for validations like that.

It was funny how many called to ask me for predictions about their life even though I always insisted on medium readings. Many people think that psychic equals fortune-teller, expecting to have their future told – but that's not what mediums do! I asked my guides to help, so we tricked them. When they would ask a question about whether their house would sell or not, my guides would bring forward their spirit people and I would say something like, 'well, the house will sell, but I feel you have a mother in spirit'. Then the healing could begin again. This was the real reason I was there, not for the life questions that could be answered easily just by looking closely at your own feelings.

We were really having a great time on radio and I was learning a lot about the people I worked with. One Monday after the show, I decided to give all the office staff a free reading and they loved it! It was a long but enjoyable day. I also learned that Ronnie was born with four baby teeth which made me look at him a little differently - my thoughts went out to his mother whom he assured me handled it all in her stride. Yes, those were wonderful days at Hot 91. Chrissy was always wanting me to give her something, anything, just a little bit of psychic stuff and Ronnie often teased me, accusing me of not caring about them. How was it that two disc-jockeys who had a medium reading on their breakfast show were not getting read?! I was not able to get any spirit through for them, although I did try without them knowing....

Around that time, I started to notice something else happening. My shows on the Sunshine Coast always sold out, and I'd actually had someone come up to me in the street hugging and thanking me for all the good work I was doing. Wow, I thought, this is getting a little weird. But it was nice that people were hugging me for doing other people's readings. How wonderful for some people to do that. I was getting a lot of work on the Sunshine Coast at this stage and was spending more and more time there. I would head up for about three days of readings every two weeks. My life was very busy.

Chapter 14

Mothers, Mates and the Medium

In May 2005, my mum came to watch a show at Ballina for the first time. I must admit that I was a little nervous with mum in the audience, but the show was a huge success. I made time to go down the following July to do private readings. It was around this time that I hired Mandy, young Tash's mum. The very same Mandy that had walked into my office a broken woman after her young daughter had tragically drowned in a dam. It was funny the way that I came about hiring her. It had started with one of my follow-up visits just to see if Mandy was ok, whilst visiting my mum in Stanthorpe. I was having coffee with Mandy when her daughter came through.

"Mandy, the hospital is going to offer you a job in the office," I told her.

"No way! I'm going to be a nurse?" Mandy replied.

"Oh, that's funny," I told her, "because Tash just told me that you were actually going to be training for office-work which they will pay for."

"No way," said Mandy.

"The funny thing is, Tash says you are going to be working for me!"

Mandy exclaimed that she would not leave Stanthorpe.

"Funny," I said, not entirely convinced myself at that stage, "because that is what Tash thinks."

That was two years ago.

Three months later, Mandy called.

"Guess what? They have offered me a job in the office at the hospital and they are paying for me to do a full administration course!"

Well, the rest is now history and as it turns out, Mandy has an office in Stanthorpe where she does all the 'behind-the-scene' work. Who would have thought? I did. And so did Tash.

After that, it was off to Darwin, which I must say was an excellent experience. I love Darwin and its laid-back lifestyle. Even though it has a very hot climate, it seems that the town is in permanent party-mode. I've seen people walking the streets of Darwin with beers in their hands, almost like they're at some giant permanent barbeque. I met a family in Darwin whom I consider to this day to be one of the most unlucky in the land. This poor family had lost their son in 2002 to a heart attack, their daughter in 2003 to cancer and their other son in 2004 to murder. All of these children were in their twenties. As you can imagine, it was a very sad and grief-stricken family. I was, and still am amazed at the strength of this tragic family and should they read this, please know that I wish them strength and love, and sincerely hope for light in their lives. I only wish that I could have helped them a little more. It proved to me that no matter how bad things get in your life, there is always someone else much, much worse off.

After the Darwin trip, I was off to Cairns and this time I took a personal assistant, my mum.

Mum had not been back to Cairns since 1977 and was longing to have another look, so I took the opportunity to make this dream real. It was there that I met a woman called Margaret whose sister had been involved in a murder-suicide years before in the Atherton Tablelands. It had been deemed a murder-suicide but a lot of questions still remained. The reading was accurate in details but the question of whether or not it was a suicide plagues me to this day. I feel a little differently now than I did during the actual reading, and believe that a third party was involved. Life as a medium was proving to be frustrating when questions like this arose.

Shortly after I came home from Cairns, I went to Ballina to do the private readings I had arranged. I met a woman called Kim and her lovely spirit daughter Brooke. Kim has kindly allowed me to publish her story and her views on the reading.

The reading of Kim Moore Evans on the 5th July 2005

Brooke died tragically in a car accident on the 6th July 2003. She was a passenger in the back seat of a car which lost control and crashed head-on with a semi-trailer. Everyone in the car died instantly, all at precisely the same time and of the same injuries, a broken brain stem. This information was given to me by the Coroner's report.

From the time of losing Brooke, I have wanted to believe that she was with me in spirit but until you have been shown proof, there is always doubt about the afterlife. Recently, my future husband and I were looking for a venue to be married in, when I think Brooke tried to make contact for the first time. The feelings which overcame me I cannot describe, other than to say it felt like Brooke led me by the hand to this wonderful spiritual place. This was the closest I had felt to her since losing her. As it turned out, the woman who owned the venue was a medium as well as a celebrant. We ended up being married there, but I didn't know if I was ready to try and contact Brooke just yet.

A couple of months later, my boss Karen told me about a seminar being held by Charmaine at the Ballina RSL and we decided to go. We were amazed at what we heard and decided to book a reading. From there, I was finally able to make contact with my beautiful girl once again.

I believe that Brooke tried to make contact once but didn't succeed and then made it possible for Karen to see the advertisement in the paper which led us here to this reading.

Brooke's Reading, 5th July 2005

Charmaine: I am getting a smoker through first... someone above you... a father figure

Kim: My ex- father-in -law passed

Charmaine: He is saying that he has someone younger with him and is giving me a 'J' initial

David: My father's name was John and he is in spirit

Charmaine: I am now getting a pain in my head. Like a tumour, stroke or car accident. They are all over the place and seem to be hustling to get in, they have no manners.

Kim: I have someone who passed in a car accident

Charmaine: Is this like someone to your side like a sister.

Kim: No, it is my daughter.

Charmaine: Oh, this might explain why I have so much confusion, she is wanting to come through and I have several energies who want the same thing.

Charmaine: That would be why your father-in-law was telling me he had someone younger with him here.

Charmaine: She is telling me that there is a birthday right now like her birthday, your birthday or someone else that is close. I mean right now.

Kim: Yes

Charmaine: She just wants to say "Happy Birthday" to them, it must be right now though, does that make sense?

Kim: It is my birthday in two days' time and her Dad's today.

Charmaine: She wishes to acknowledge the 'R' name, is that her Dad?

Kim: No, it's her uncle, Russell.

Charmaine: Please say hello to him

Charmaine: She is telling me that someone fell
pregnant around the time she crossed,
her uncle?

Kim: It's to do with her dad's son.

Charmaine: She is giving me a 'C' or 'K' name - a
female, I think

Kim: Yes, that is Crystal

Charmaine: Is that her name? Because if it is, that
is the same as my daughter who also
passed in a car accident.

Kim: No, that is the girl who fell pregnant.

Charmaine: I really want to put the colour purple
here, feel that is your daughters
colour

Kim: Yes

Charmaine: She is telling me that there is a 'B'
name like Brianna, no it is a Br name
- would it be Brooke?

Kim: That is her name

Charmaine: She is only a tiny girl, isn't she?

Kim: Yes

Charmaine: She is only young, isn't she?

Kim: Yes

Charmaine: She is little then?

Kim: No, she is a teenager - she is just
small-framed.

Charmaine: She gave a 6 , is she 16?

Kim:	Yes
Charmaine:	She is talking about shoes, do you understand?
Kim:	Yes
Charmaine:	Why am I thinking of caramel tarts right now?
Kim:	Because we used to get caramel rings from the cake shop.
Charmaine:	She indicates that you just got married.
Kim:	Yes
Charmaine:	She says that she was there in spirit. She tells me that there was a blue colour at the wedding party.
Kim:	Yes a blue /purple colour.
Charmaine:	She tells me you had her photo at the wedding
Kim:	Yes
Charmaine:	She has dark hair
Kim:	Yes
Charmaine:	She is discussing a tattoo
Kim:	My other daughter has one.
Charmaine:	She indicates that the accident was alcohol or drug related
Kim:	Yes
Charmaine:	She is telling me that no one got in trouble for the accident

Kim:	They all passed over
Charmaine:	She is telling me that there are two more besides her
Kim:	Yes
Charmaine:	She is telling me that a young male was driving, with fair hair, surfy look. She seems to be keen on him, he is very protective of her. He has his arm around her. He is very tall. Good looking but skinny. He was the one that was on drugs. She is giving me an 'S' name
Kim:	Yes, his name is Steven
Charmaine:	He wants to say sorry
Kim:	I want to forgive him, but I can't
Charmaine:	It takes a long time
Charmaine:	This is not that long ago - she is giving me a 6, is it 6 months or years?
Kim:	It is the 6th day of the month
Charmaine:	She is giving me a 2 now
Kim:	It is two years - tomorrow the 6th
Charmaine:	OMG! your husband's birthday today, her anniversary tomorrow and your birthday on the following day.
Kim:	Yes, I feel she wanted us back together and this was the way she could do it.
Charmaine:	She is telling me that you have journals

Kim: Yes, I have hers.

Charmaine: She is telling me that she got in the wedding photos. She is telling me that she was not in school and that there is a reference to someone from school who has just given her some acknowledgment in the year-book or something.

Kim: Yes

Charmaine: She is giving me the colour orange like an orange outfit, I cant imagine her in it or it may be something that you have.

Kim: No way - not me or her

D Josh nearly bought you an orange skirt today for you birthday

Charmaine: Did he? And you never knew that Kim?

Kim: No!

Charmaine: That's her way, David, of letting you know that she likes you and was with you during the shopping today.

Charmaine: She gives me the impression of being the fashion queen

Kim: She made her own fashion

Charmaine: I feel she was very game with fashion.

Kim: Yes, she wore short skirts with Ugg boots before it was in fashion, and I told her she was not allowed to go out with me dressed like that.

Charmaine:	That is the fashion now. Two years ahead! She wants to prove a point here that she was on the ball.
Charmaine:	She tells me that she was born in April, so she is an Aries..What a beautiful child !
Kim:	Yes, she is.

Around that time, I received the best news that I had heard in a long time. My eldest son, Alan, who at one time had never wanted to live with me again, asked if he could move back in. It seemed that for the first time in the six years since their father had taken my boys, they were really missing living with me. Perhaps my new outlook on life had slowly but surely brought back the mother they loved. I was no longer quick to judge or become angry. I had learned, through the many books that spirit had directed me to, how to accept myself and understand that the mistakes I had made were just that: mistakes. I was finally learning to love myself again and it is true that if you do not love yourself, then others do not find it easy to do so. My boys had been saying for a while that they wanted to live with me, especially my youngest son, Jack, but he always had. To have my oldest son actually state that he was moving in was perhaps one of the greatest moments of my life. It seemed the universe was smiling at me and that perhaps I was receiving another chance.

Alan's return was also a big step for me as a mother, going back to the school routine and so on. My son was in grade eleven and was very capable, so I knew we could work it out. Jack also wanted to live with me, but his father flatly said no. It would have been difficult anyway as I did have a very heavy touring schedule coming up, and an eleven-year-old would need constant supervision. It was a happy time, but tinged with some sadness as I would dearly have loved to have had both boys. It has however worked out wonderfully with both boys appreciating each other even more now that they only met up every two weeks. My son, Alan, is the one responsible for my website and I have done everything I can to help him on his way to becoming a webmaster. With each step of this journey, the rewards were coming not only in my personal life but also in the ability to help others connect with the children they had lost. Working with spirit is perhaps the ultimate way to receiving fulfilment in this life. It is to me anyway. Of course it has its frustrations, but ultimately, if you do decide to embrace the universal way of life, it definitely pays off in rewards such as love, acceptance and happiness.

It was with this new found happiness that I walked into my next show at the Kawana Waters Surf Club. This was another *Girl in a Million* function and one we had to turn people away from, as we had sold way over the tickets that the seating allowed. I first laid eyes on my wonderful friend Peter that night. Yes, there's that name again. I remember seeing him sitting about three rows back, and the look on his face after each reading. He was also the one who rode past me on his motorised push-bike at the end of the night calling out, 'Goodnight and thank you very much for the show!'. I had the chance to meet him in person a few weeks later at a private session and what a night to remember! First off, I got a phone call from Mandy.

She was laughing her head off. It seemed that Peter was incredibly late and she said he was beside himself. You see, Peter is a gay man and everything is done with flair and fluster. He turned up half an hour late. It seemed he had gone back to the Surf Club for his reading. As the taxi pulled up, I could see him wrapped in a scarf and huge jacket. He had a big bunch of flowers (to say sorry) and was waving frantically from the cab window. I could not help but smile.

He was the best. He air-kissed my cheek and exclaimed how sorry he was, 'darling'. Would I ever forgive him? He has to be the first gay man I have fallen in love with on the spot. I felt so warm in his presence. We sat down for the reading and his mother came through immediately. She was wonderful to work with and told me her name was Phyllis. She told me all about her son and how close they were. She told how she had died unexpectedly and how unhappy Peter had been without her. She told me of his two little dogs, Gracie and Steffi, and how they were his kids. Peter had tears rolling down his cheeks. It was exactly what he needed. We both got so much out of that night and am very happy to say we both gained a friend for life.

After that, it was back to Emerald and back to my good friends, Gay and Vic. Now, there was a funny mix! Gay is one of the most spiritual people you could ever hope to meet and Vic is a typical hardworking Australian male with little or no obvious spiritual beliefs. For some strange reason, he has taken a liking to me and is happy to have me in his home every time I go to Emerald. Unfortunately, their eldest son, David had committed suicide six years before and while Vic works far too much to bury his pain, Gay meditates and reads everything she can on the afterlife. I had met her during a phone reading twelve months before, and she invited me up to do some readings for her friends and have the first show of the year. Vic had actually let me read him at that time, decided that I was 'ok', and to my absolute delight, greeted me upon my return with a kiss on the cheek and a hug. Gay has never stopped marvelling at the way he has accepted me and my "mumbo jumbo". She feels it is a step in the right direction. I hope so. Once again, the show at Emerald was a big one and a great one. I also met Ben's friends and family and was able to convince his mate that the spirit world did in fact exist. You may remember that Ben walked into the first Emerald reading in his spirit form with a slab of Rum and cola on his shoulder. I love Emerald and will surely find myself back there again in the future. I think these small country towns are the places that often need the most healing.

It was just after this time that I went back to Bundaberg. A few days before I was due to leave, I received a phone call from a woman who was frantic about her brother. He had apparently not been seen for three weeks. He had called his brother and told him that he was going to end his own life. This often cruel world had got the better of him. I was not sure what to do, so I offered a phone reading for free as it was an area that I was unfamiliar with. The reading was a great one with all the other family members coming through. Then at the end of the reading, I had another spirit. It seemed to be the brother that she was so worried about. I was able to describe him, his house and very accurately the circumstances of the day in question during which he had disappeared. I was very upset, as I did not want him to be in this reading. As it turned out, he was living in Gympie at the time he disappeared and that was on my way to Bundaberg. I offered to drop by on my way through and meet his sister there to see if I could get anything else. As I drove down the lonely country road that he lived in, I didn't need to be told which house was his as I recognised it immediately. It was exactly as I had seen it in my vision. My heart was pounding. I wasn't sure if I was ready for this. I had seen the TV program *Sensing Murder* and this seemed to be straight out of it. It was eerie. I met his family and we sat in this poor broken man's house and talked. We went to the location that I had described over the phone – the place that his family knew he had last gone to. We did not find him, but I left that place with such sadness that I cried the entire way to Bundaberg. I could feel that man's spirit with me in the house and I was overwhelmed with sadness. I am not sure to this day if they found him as I have lost touch. I have decided to stick with my work of only contacting spirits that people know have definitely passed.

Chapter 15

The Show Must Go On

When I got back home, I called my new friend, Peter. I just couldn't get him out of my mind. He was delighted as it was his birthday the day before, so we figured it was his mum that had made me call. He was so funny. He told me how he had had his eyelashes tinted a few days before.

"And then, Charmaine, I went to the Kawana Waters Bowls club for the bistro dinner. Well Charmaine, on the way, the petrol cap came off my motorised push bike and I got petrol all over my hand bag!" he informed me dramatically. I was laughing out loud by now.

"There I was, Charmaine, standing in line at the bistro when the woman in front of me said to her friend, 'Smells like a truckie behind me'. Well, Charmaine, she turned around and took one look at me and my tinted eyelashes and said, 'You're no truckie.'"

By this time, I was in fits!

"I don't know, Charmaine. The people at the Kawana Waters Bowls Club just don't appreciate glamour when they see it!"

How I loved this man! I promised to catch up the following month when I was due to do a show at the Maroochydore RSL. I mean, he was like a happy pill when I talked to him, so I have affectionately dubbed him my 'Peter Pill'. Whenever I am feeling down, my mum says, "Why not get a 'Peter Pill'?"

I went down to see my mum after that for the September holidays. My son Jack loved his grandmother's house as it was a beautiful place set on ninety-three acres with so much to do for an eleven-year-old. My eldest son had long ago stopped coming with us. It was great to get a break from the heavy touring schedule I had put myself through. After that break was the Sunshine Coast show. I had decided to drop in and see my 'Peter Pill' and see if he would straighten my hair for the evening. I had invited my friend Joanne up to see the show and to take a few photos to use in the book. I set off to Peter's place before meeting Jo. Well, he was up in arms as he took me on the 'Grand Tour'. He introduced me to his rat, which he calls 'Mouse' - but you must say it in a rounded voice, as in 'Mowse'. As we toured the house, we came to the back door and there were two of the most pathetic looking, recently styled and cut, shivering and shaking Maltese Terriers. They were peering anxiously through the back door. "And those," spat Pete "...are the bitches!" I couldn't help but laugh.

"That one is Gracie and the other is Steffie. Oh, Charmaine, you would not believe what they have done, they are in disgrace and they are staying there until they learn their lesson," my 'Peter Pill' continued. "You see, Charmaine, I only have a little piece of chocolate occasionally and I like to place it on my bedside table - you know, just to have when I am feeling a little peckish. Well, can you believe it, those bitches took the chocolate and ate it all - foil, the lot - and they got it all over my

Queen Anne bedspread. Oh Charmaine, it looked like I have been menstruating all over the bed. I cannot think what has come over them." I was in fits of laughter as I looked at these tiny villains, shaking and clearly upset that their Daddy did not love them anymore. We finished the 'Grand Tour', with me laughing out loud at the thought of Peter menstruating. After that, it was on to the hair straightening. You see, he had been a hairdresser. Afterwards, we had coffee and discussed my upcoming photo shoot. Peter looked at me and his eyes widened. "Cream!" he exclaimed suddenly. "Oh Charmaine, I can just picture you in cream, you would look like an Angel!" Then he got up and proceeded to strike some model poses for me showing me how to stand in front of the show that night.

"You could stand like this - and like this." he said, all the while striking poses. I was in hysterics. It was time to leave, unfortunately. We said our farewells in a flurry of air kisses.

Needless to say, I *did* forget to pose that night but something extraordinary happened with the photos. I don't stand still for long, so it's difficult to get a good shot. The show had a special magic that night with many connections taking place.

"So, what did you end up with?" I asked Jo as I stirred the coffees back at the motel.

"Not much," she said, "except for this one of you on stage - with your guide..."

I thought she was joking, but sure enough, standing beside me in the photo I could clearly see a male figure - beard, aviator glasses and all. When you look at it closely you can see how it has happened – on the longer exposure, my own movements had blurred to make an illusion. But however it happened on the technical side, the resulting image clearly showed the Peter who stands beside me in spirit - my guide. It was so eerie. We couldn't believe it.

The next morning, it was off to the beach to shoot more photos. Believe me when I say that I am useless when it comes to putting on make up. We called 'Peter Pill'.

"Oh Charmaine, I am much too busy and I have an electrician here," 'Peter Pill' lamented. "The poor man, Charmaine, he doesn't know where to look. He is a straight man and here I am prancing around in my satin short wrap and fluffy slippers. I think I better go and change."

The photo shoot went well. Although pose as I might, I just can't understand why the camera does not make me look like Alyssa Milano. Damned disappointing!

It was a sad time too, as Hot 91 called to tell me that I would not be needed until December as they were in survey time and felt that they needed to play more music. That's radio for you.

I headed off to North Queensland. Because of my earlier trip, I had arranged to do another show circuit and private readings. This time, I was on the road for almost a month. I had contacted Sea FM Radio in Rockhampton in preparation for my first show and had connected with a lovely lady called Anna who immediately got me a spot on air. The trip in April had been a sell-out due to a great press write-up and this trip was proving to be the same. The Rockhampton show had almost twice the audience of the first one, and the crowd was anxious. I know they all wanted to be read, but with shows so big, it was getting harder to please everyone. I was into my 'radio reads' (quick reads) when I asked a blonde woman who she would like to talk to. She asked for her son. I had a little trouble identifying how he had died but knew it was due to something around the head area. This woman was carrying a lot of guilt, as most parents do, and it needed to be alleviated.

Charmaine: Your son is telling me he died due to something in the head area - I can't tell what it is

Listener: He died from a cerebral haemorrhage.

(This was very unusual for a person this age. I had him picked for late teens/early twenties)

Charmaine: Your son is not alone, he has your father with him

Listener: Yes

Charmaine: He was a heavy smoker, in fact that is what was responsible for taking him away.

Listener: Yes

Charmaine: He liked to sing, in fact he is singing '*and I wanna go home*'. I think it is the Banana Boat song.

Listener: Oh my gosh! He always sang that song!

I was still trying to get my head around the fact that they made me sing in front of two hundred people! I gave her a heap of names which evade me right now, and she was one happy woman. I really hope that it helped.

The next reading, I shall never forget. It was an elderly lady in her seventies. She was dressed head-to-toe with the elegance that modern women have not been able to capture. She was a tiny woman and when I asked her to stand up, she did so with poise and such a beautiful straight back. She spoke clearly into the microphone and when I asked her who she would like to contact, she politely asked for her mother. The first thing I saw was a nursing home.

Charmaine:	Your mother passed in a nursing home
Lady:	No
Charmaine:	She is giving me the initial E.. and says Edie
Lady:	No, but my Aunt passed recently and her name was Eenie
Charmaine:	Did this lady pass in a Home?
Lady:	Yes
Charmaine:	She seems to be taking the mother's position
Lady:	Thats right, she raised me
Charmaine:	I have someone else here, a woman, this is your mother. You were very young when she passed
Lady:	Yes
Charmaine:	She passed in an accident
Lady:	Yes
Charmaine:	She is giving me a P, like Phylis

Lady: That was my mother's name..

(The lady reached for her husband's hand at that point.)

Charmaine: She tells me that you finally wear her
                  ring. You didn't have it for a long while

Lady: Yes

Charmaine: She wants you to know that she has
                  watched over you all these years.

And with that the spirit sent love and pulled back. After the reading, the elegant lady came up to me and explained that her mother had been killed in a train accident involving the whole family. They had actually been hit by a train and only she and her father had survived. She was eighteen months old. She had been raised by her Aunt Eenie and had just recently renewed her vows with her husband. She had her old wedding ring and her mother's ring melted and made into one. She thanked me repeatedly and in that moment, I thanked God for this beautiful gift that brings hope and closure to so many.

I stayed for another few days and conducted private readings. Then it was off to Mackay. Once again, the radio station Hot FM was happy to have me back, this time for the two days leading up to the show. The show was sold out and we had to turn many away. Well, well, is all I can say! Once again, I fell victim to my own hormones. In the middle of the third reading, I felt myself menstruating heavily. In fact, I was getting dizzy and after that, everything went askew. What a dilemma! Women really do get it all a little harder - if only I was a bloke at that moment. Everything was offbeat. It's difficult too, because you hardly want to announce to a whole audience that you have your period. I ended up staying back and doing little one-on-ones for an hour but I was very upset. I mean, all of those people had paid and it was a total fizzle. What could I do? I started the twelve hour trip home but by the time I had driven one hour, I had arranged to do a free show for all who had attended. The radio station told everyone about it and I felt much happier. I spent the weekend with my youngest boy, as he was why I had driven home, and I flew back up the following Monday. The next show was a success with about one hundred turning up. People started telling me how they were sure that the people in front of them had received *their* reading during the 'washout' show. Why didn't they say something at the time? I now make a firm point at letting people know that this may happen and should this be the case, to speak up.

It was in Mackay that I first started doing readings with a national radio show called *Nelly at Night*. It is broadcast from Gold FM on the Gold Coast to forty regional stations Australia-wide. This was great, as we conducted the show with conference phone. That meant I could be anywhere in Australia and do the show from my bedroom. It was amazing really to think that people all over Australia were listening to me and getting the opportunity to ring up and be connected. I may have lost Hot 91 but I had gained a great opportunity with *Nelly at Night*. It was perfect timing too. I was already planning an Australian tour visiting outback towns, and now I had regional radio coverage. Did my guides love me or what?

I finished off my work at Mackay and then had a lovely wedding to go to on the Saturday. Now, this is where it gets a little weird. You see, the day after the wedding was the 23rd of October and I was booked to do a show at the Townsville RSL at 2pm. Whilst Mandy was booking my flights and rooms on the 27th of August, she asked me if I would like to fly up to Townsville on the Sunday. The plane would have left Mackay at 12 noon to arrive at 1pm. Well, that sounded fine to me. I was about to agree when my guide, Peter, said, "Hire a car." Huh? I thought about it and thought that I would be arriving at the RSL at about 1.40pm - it all sounded ok to me. But again he said, "Hire a car or you will not make it in time for the show." What? I asked Mandy to look into car hire and it turned out it would be more expensive than the plane flight. I was about to go ahead with the plane when Peter insisted again on me hiring the car. Ok then. I told Mandy to hire a car.

The day of the show arrived. I set off at 6am to make the long four hour drive to Townsville. Everything went well. I got to the show in time and asked where the manager was. He called me shortly afterwards and explained that he had been waiting at the airport for his parents. He finally arrived shortly before two and it seemed his parents still had not arrived. The plane did not in fact arrive in Townsville until 2.10pm. There had been a medical emergency in Mackay and the plane was delayed for that reason... What really freaked me out was the fact that my guides had known on the 27th of August that there would be a medical emergency on the 23rd of October. I mean, is everything written down in one great big diary in the afterlife? I think so.

This really made me believe in fate even more than I had before.

I had a great time at the Townsville show and once again, stayed a few days to conduct readings. I met a young mother who had to watch her young son die of a mystery disease. He came through wonderfully. His name was Ryan. The young woman told me about a volunteer group called the *Compassionate Friends*. This organisation had told her about me. The *Compassionate Friends* are parents who have lost children help other parents who have lost children get through the black days of grief. What a wonderful group. I made a note to contact them when I got home to see if there was a way we could work together and raise funds for their organisation. I had done a lot of work with the *Girl in a Million Quest* and was now looking for new groups to work with. I was also approaching *Bravehearts*, a support group for victims of child sexual abuse. Long ago, when I had decided to change my life, my guides, who I then thought were people in this life, had asked me what I wanted to do. I had said that I wanted to help kids who were physically, emotionally and sexually abused. You see, in my time in the murky world of drugs, I had met many of these kids. It was heartbreaking. I could not get over how badly treated they were, so I vowed to help them one day if I could. I had once applied for a youth worker certificate course, but did not have enough money to pay for it. It was after that that this crazy life of a medium became apparent. I realise now that I am able to help in a positive manner, by allowing people to use my shows to raise funds. So I was now to work with two groups.

I flew home from Townsville and contacted both groups. *Bravehearts* jumped at the chance and I invited them to my next show on the Gold Coast so they could see exactly what I was doing. This time, I was giving the entire proceeds of three shows to each charity. It was up to them to find the venue and secure as much free publicity as they could. I promised to help where I could by promoting their shows on the radio and in any newspaper article. I was also planning to take their promotional pamphlets and fundraising products to offer for sale at all of my shows. *Why not help as many as you could on the journey?* This was my main thought. The next thing on my list was to ring *Compassionate Friends*. I spoke to a lady named Marion and did a little reading for her over the phone. She promised to get back to me after the next monthly meeting and let me know.

The show on the Gold Coast was next and I was able to broadcast this on *Nelly at Night*. It was a wonderful show with two spirits that kept hogging the limelight. I mean, they *did not* want to get off. Both were Dads and they loved a chat. Both their families ended up squirming uncomfortably in their seats as once again Dad took the mike, so to speak. One thing I have learned is to just let them go. I really have no choice. It was funny. The night before the show I was sitting outside in my meditation. No fancy 'Green Rooms' for us Australian mediums. Once, I even changed in a toilet block at a garage and had to put my other shoes down to walk on as the floor was wet. Anyway, I heard this spirit telling me how he loved to dance and that he used to go on cruises in life. He also talked about a big brass bell. I thought the messages may have been for my two friends Emily and Karen from their father, so I remembered them for after the show. However, it was one of the 'persistent fathers' that had been speaking to me and when he came back, I relayed word for word what he had told me: the bell, the dance, the cruises; the fact that he was from the military. His daughter just nodded and once again, I marvelled at the strength of some spirits to be able to give me so much information before a reading. The poor woman was most embarrassed as each time I tried to read another her father would take me back to her. It was all good though as this was spirit love in its purest form. This was what people had come to see. Well, needless to say *Bravehearts* was very excited about coming on board and immediately set about organising their first show.

The next show was the Remembrance Day show for the *Girl in a Million Quest*. It was to be my last show for the diggers, although I probably would do one each year for them on this special day.

To this point, I had raised sixteen thousand dollars for them and really wanted to help the other fundraising causes so close to my heart. I will be forever grateful to Donna Regget and the other girls for helping me understand the best way to conduct shows and also for introducing me to radio. It seemed strange that it was only a year ago that I sat next to Ashley Mac at the *Girl in a Million* presentations where he had invited me to do readings on air. Now, I was a regular on a national radio show and about to embark on my first Australian Tour. Everything was falling so well into place. We already had fifty-four venues ready for the next year and now it was all about to start. I had also received the news that I was voted *Australian Psychic of the Year* for 2005 by the *Australian*

Psychics Association. This association was working hard to promote positive guidelines for our rapidly growing field. Yes, I had certainly come a long way in such a short three years. I ventured down to Coffs Harbour and Wauchope in New South Wales to test the southern waters. I tried advertising on television for the first time. It was also the first time in nineteen years that I was going to see my daughter's cross. Yes, it had been hard to take that step. If Crystal had lived, she would now be twenty-four years old.

Epilogue

So here I am at the Kempsey cemetery on the 24th of November 2005. What a journey my life has been! I know I have only just begun the next leg. I know I have been voted *Australian Psychic of the Year 2005*, but have been unable to tell anyone until the formal announcement is made. What an honour for a girl who always seemed to get it wrong! Somehow it all turned out right. What have I learned in the past years of this life? I know one thing: I wouldn't change one step of the journey. Even the bad bits were necessary. They have shaped me, made me learn, taught me about judgment and forgiveness. In hindsight, it seems that my life was tailor-made to suit the modern day psychic medium. I mean, how could I know this society unless I lived it? Did my guides (and maybe even myself) set my life to include so many pitfalls and lessons so that I could be a teacher in this life?

As I look down at the small cross, I realise once and for all that my daughter has never left me. All I am feeling is annoyed at the bad spelling. I have sensed her presence for the past five years very intensely. It has been my realisation that she did not leave at all. This is my mission, and my daughter, my brother, my father and my grandparents have all been major partners in this journey. Without their tragic losses, would I be writing this story or going around the country to reunite those in this life with those who have crossed over? I do not think so. They have helped me understand grief; they have taught me forgiveness and opened my eyes to the reality of love in its purest form of spirit. Without their constant presence and that of my beloved guides, I do not know if I would ever have survived the ordeals that I insisted on putting myself through.

The drinking, the drugs and the self-abuse were all part of this journey. The whole lot has taught me lessons that I could never have gleaned from textbooks. I have been to the lowest depths that society has to offer with my foray into the world of amphetamines and have seen things that no eyes should ever see, but I learned so much whilst down there. From that, I learned that there are people in society who need help because they will not or cannot help themselves; hence my work with *Bravehearts* and the *Compassionate Friends*. I do not think for a moment that I was not touched or even hurt by that world, but the most important thing is that I survived and believed in myself enough to get up and get out, and once I had my breath back, to do what I could to help.

This world can be so selfish, but the lesson I have learned is that we all have so much to give. Those who gave me back my life, after I thought I was ready to give up and die, have been the greatest givers of all. They are of course my guides and my family in spirit. They have taught me how to hear, see and feel them with every waking moment; and the whole way, I was given choices on what I wanted to do. It was my choice to be a medium and I do believe that I was always destined to be one. It is not the easiest of lives. Most people either roll their eyes or ask for a reading when I tell them what I do. I have long ago given up on trying to 'prove' myself. I realise it is not me that they challenge, it's the whole concept of the afterlife. I had to learn not to take everything so personally.

I have received but a few human guides along the way. My friend Janet's teachings helped me understand and then go on to format her teachings into the *Spirit Talk* seminar; Mandy, my very patient and understanding assistant (may her patience last forever!), and last but by not least, my mother, who with much patience and knowing has been my central support system my entire life.

The life of a medium can be very lonely. You have to learn to live with yourself and understand that your old friends may not understand you or the work you do anymore. Some step back, and it can seem that every conversation you have revolves around this never-ending work. There are many that need your gift and many that you will never meet. The ones that I have met, I know have been touched or changed in a little way by the process. Process is the best word, because the whole life/death wheel is a process. In these modern days, we have forgotten that death is a natural process we must all pass through. We take it all so personally; we have forgotten that this life is part of one enormous journey where we all fit, and that we all have a part to play. It is my belief that the universe has woken up the mediums so that we can once again understand that we are merely spirit having a human experience.

Why are we mediums on stage? There are those who believe it is all a rip off, and that we are preying on the vulnerability of those who are newly bereaved. I do not think these people have even given it a go, or maybe they do not need to. Even people in our own profession think that those of us who choose to take the show on the road are wrong. I challenge these mediums to see how many people do change in one show and how essential the information that is given in these shows is in helping a grieving world to heal.

Medium, me? Who would have thought that my life would have gone this far? Who could have guessed that so many would be a recipient of the gift I have been given? People ask me about heaven and if I know what it is like. Well, I get the impression that heaven is only another dimension, unseen to our human eyes, that coexists with the world in which we live. We only have to open our eyes to the ever present signs to know it is there. Live in the moment and love this life, these are the secrets.

It has been a journey and one I embrace daily. It has caused me to cry, to laugh and to love.

I have never been so aware of how important it is to think right and to try to do the right thing in every waking moment.

I am an Australian medium and I am happy to be one. I chose to do this work in the hope to help many who have had to view their child in a coffin or watch their parents take their last breath. And also to help people gain an understanding that there is more to this life than meets the eye. To help people understand that all is good in the afterlife and it is there that we will meet and continue our journey once again. Our work gives hope to a hopeless world. And may it always do so.

Yes, I have seen a rainbow
fall from the sky.
I have seen angels lose their wings.
I have seen too many little ones die.
I have watched my dreams disappear
into a blood red sea.
And I am telling you these things have affected me,
but I have always believed in me.

Spirit Child (Ode to Crystal)

The rainbow colour surrounds you
The sun, it lights up your face
It's been a while since I found you
You've gone to another place
You're my spirit child, child so fine
Sweet Spirit child, child of mine

The mountain air is your perfume
Crystal's the sound of your voice
You've got the beauty of a rose bloom
You never had any choice
Poor, poor baby
My poor poor child

My sweet, sweet spirit child,
sweet child, so kind
When I lost you baby,
You know I lost my mind
Been so long since I've seen you
I never said my goodbye

Your heartbeat still lives within me
Your laughter rings in my ears
When I think of what could be
You wipe away my tears
Good kind sweet baby
Sweet spirit child of mine.

For more information about Charmaine Wilson
please visit: www.spiritwhispers.org

CPSIA information can be obtained
at www.ICGtesting.com
Printed in the USA
LVHW012207260723
753604LV00010B/216